The Married Man's Mentor

Lucas Lovibond

**Andrews McMeel
Publishing, LLC**
Kansas City

The Married Man's Mentor copyright © 2007 by Andrews McMeel Publishing.
All rights reserved. Printed in the United States of America. No part of this book may
be used or reproduced in any manner whatsoever without written permission
except in the case of reprints in the context of reviews. For information, write
Andrews McMeel Publishing, LLC, an Andrews McMeel Universal company,
4520 Main Street, Kansas City, Missouri 64111.

07 08 09 10 11 RR2 10 9 8 7 6 5 4 3 2 1

ISBN-13: 978-0-7407-6371-7
ISBN-10: 0-7407-6371-7

Library of Congress Control Number: 2006931347

www.andrewsmcmeel.com

ATTENTION: SCHOOLS AND BUSINESSES
Andrews McMeel books are available at quantity discounts with bulk purchase
for educational, business, or sales promotional use. For information, please write to:
Special Sales Department, Andrews McMeel Publishing, LLC,
4520 Main Street, Kansas City, Missouri 64111.

*There is no relation of life in which it is more necessary
to cultivate a certain faculty of imagination than
in marriage. You must accustom yourself to look at things,
to a certain extent, from your wife's point of view.*

Lucas Lovibond, *The Married Man's Mentor*, 1899

The first time I held this book I made a handwritten note: "*This one* isn't just boxed but also wrapped in tissue paper inside the box!"

Even at the British Library, where I've had five-hundred-year-old first editions on my desk, *The Married Man's Mentor* looked like something rather special.

The tissue unfolded to reveal a handsome, dark volume with a gold-embossed title and a swirling silver decoration very much characteristic of its epoch. The book had been published by one Thomas Burleigh of London in 1899.

So far nothing too much out of the ordinary. I'd been researching late Victorian marriage manuals for my novel, wanting to know the expectations of a bride and a groom of the times. I'd found plenty of coy advice for young women. Certainly, this was the first book specifically geared to men, but the design was still decidedly feminine or at least aimed at the female eye. I supposed that then, as now, it was the women who bought most of the books.

But as soon as I started reading *The Married Man's Mentor*, I knew I had discovered something unusually good. For a start, the writing was far more stylish than most of the marriage manuals I had read (many dozens at that point). There was both a freshness to the way the writer expressed himself and a delightfully ironic undercurrent. But among these pleasures was embedded so much startling good sense that I started copying down paragraphs, not for my novel, but for my own husband.

Lucas Lovibond had words of wisdom on all aspects of marriage: choice of a wife, brains versus beauty, pitfalls of the honeymoon, financial affairs. But what appealed to me most was the way in which the book dealt sensitively and directly with areas that are often blind spots for husbands—issues that seem small but which can in fact constitute huge betrayal in the hearts and minds of their wives. In all, the book was a manual about loyalty—not just physical fidelity but simple loyalty to a partner in a far wider sense, a quality not too often discussed, except in the breach. On this subject there can be an abyss between the sexes. It is not just that men flout the unwritten rules of loyalty; they just do not recognize them in the same ways that women do.

But Lucas Lovibond had grasped the importance of loyalty and was prepared to talk about it in detail, with examples. I was impressed. The writer seemed to have a unique insight into what a woman needs from her husband in order to feel secure both in his affections and in the esteem of those around her. For example:

> *Set your face firmly against all discussion of your wife, even though it be done in the very kindest manner, by your own old home circle. After all, her success or failure as a housekeeper, as a mother, and as a woman of the world, is your business.*

And:

> *More easy to deal with, perhaps, is the case when the wife is jealous of some particular woman, who is often an employee of her husband in his busines. . . . In that case it is your duty to cast aside any foolish feeling of pride and prove the groundlessness of your wife's jealousy by dismissing the employee. . . .*
>
> *After all, you must remember that your wife may have sharper eyes than you, and that she may be aware of the gossip of censorious tongues which are always ready to put the worse possible construction on the most innocent relationships.*

I read the book cover to cover, taking copious notes.

Then I turned my attention to the author. "Lucas Lovibond," a name teasingly like my own, but not one I'd heard before, ever, during years of researching nineteenth-century material. The British Library catalog revealed no other titles by this author.

I leafed back through to the front of the book. Intriguingly there was a notice beside the title page:

IN ACTIVE PREPARATION:
The Married Woman's Mentor
Servants: How to Obtain Them and How to Manage Them

Sadly, the British Library's Integrated Catalog showed no trace of the "active preparation" ever culminating in publication for those two titles.

There are many ways and means open to a researcher looking for an author. I immediately rounded up all the usual suspects in the library. The biographical stacks yielded nothing.

Surprised, I combed the electronic resources, huge databases unthinkable in the times of Mr. Lovibond and his publisher. Ponderous CD-ROMS, heavy with unimaginable burdens of fact, slowly unfurled in front of me: *The Dictionary of National Biography, Who Was Who, Literature Resource Center, Literature Online, Contemporary Authors,* and so on.

I found Beatrice Lovibond, a Victorian physician; Edward Lovibond, an eighteenth-century poet; another Edward Lovibond, this time a Victorian brewer; and Joseph William Lovibond, a physicist . . . but no Lucas.

I decided to act on a dawning hunch that "Lovibond" was a pseudonym. With such an accomplished writing style, such a confident voice, it seemed impossible that Lucas Lovibond should not have been published elsewhere and should remain unrecorded in the annals of literature.

There was another consideration behind this. Male writers are rarely shy and retiring, but a female writer might well use a male pseudonym in order to get herself published or protect her privacy. It all added up: the deep insight into female insecurity, the ladylike design of the book, the fact that a *Married Woman's Mentor* was planned as a follow-up. I was beginning to think that the name "Lucas Lovibond" hid not just a mystery writer, but a female one at that.

Back to the shelves. But *The Bibliographical History of Anonyma and Pseudonyma* made no mention of any Lovibond, nor did the other books in that section, not even the magisterial Halkett's *Dictionary of Anonymous and Pseudonymous Publications in the English Language.*

It was at this point that I decided I needed help and called on one of the librarians, something I hadn't needed to do in ten years. She ticked off all my points of research and made a quick tour of the mighty system that reveals all the library holdings in the UK. There was only one other copy of *The Married Man's Mentor*, and that was in Scotland, too far for me to go on the faint possibility of useful annotations by some unsupervised reader.

The extraordinary scarcity of copies indicated a very small printing, possibly even a private "vanity" publication. So I turned my attention to Lucas Lovibond's publisher, Thomas Burleigh. At the end of the book I found his address, 17 Cecil Court, Charing Cross. By coincidence, this was the same place where a close friend now runs London's Italian Bookshop. The publication date of 1899 suggested that Mr. Burleigh may have been that now-extinct breed of gentleman booksellers who also did a little publishing on the side.

Mr. Burleigh had eclectic tastes. His books included *Her Wild Oats: A Novel*, described by the *Daily Mail* as "audaciously original," and *Verses for Grannie Suggested by the Children*.

The English Catalog of Books (1898–1900) recorded that *The Married Man's Mentor* was published in November 1899 and that it cost two shillings and sixpence. There were no other mentions of the book in any other catalog of publication.

And that was absolutely the end of the line for Lucas Lovibond and *The Married Man's Mentor*.

I left the library, frustrated and mystified. Never had a writer been so hard to track down.

From my study at home I launched e-mails and letters to other agencies that had been helpful in the past—the British Society of Authors and similar organizations in America, just in case.

Precisely no answers came.

People always say to writers, "I suppose you do all your research on the Internet." And any good writer will answer with an emphatic

"No!" For a start, it is not reliable. Anyone can post anything up there, and they do. Except at certain highly respectable sites, there is no sifting, checking, or proofreading. I do use the Internet, but not for direct research. It is a place to start, to gather a bibliography of real books to look at.

So the Internet was one of my last ports of call. And I never did find any information about Lucas Lovibond on the Web. But there, a few weeks later, I had my one stroke of luck: a vintage copy of *The Married Man's Mentor* for sale. I ordered it immediately.

I decided it would make a wonderful (not to say useful) Christmas or birthday present for my husband.

But then I thought again. I've worked in publishing all my life, and I just knew that this book would make a perfect Christmas or birthday present for *any* husband. I remembered that the book had been published in November 1899; clearly it was an early manifestation of that successful phenomenon, the Christmas gift book. I showed it to my very enterprising editor, Patty Rice at Andrews McMeel, and she saw the potential immediately.

It is a reproduction of my own original copy that you are about to read, and I hope very much that you find it as illuminating as I did. And if anyone who reads this book has any information that might lead to the whereabouts—or even the true identity—of Lucas Lovibond, or any other works he (or she) might have written, I remain entirely intrigued.

MICHELLE LOVRIC, London, August 2006

Michelle Lovric is the author of three historical novels and the editor of numerous anthologies.

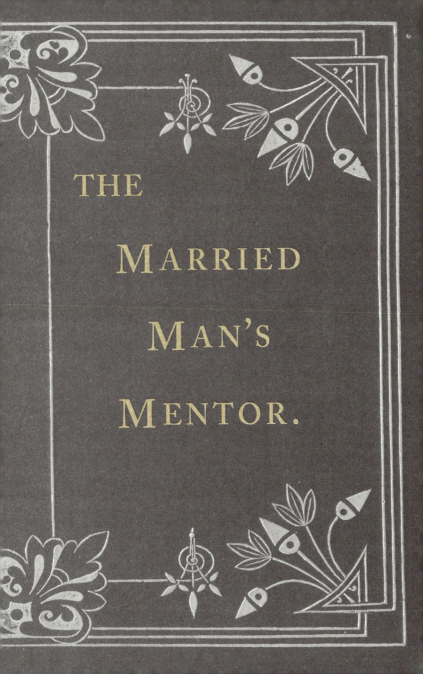

IN ACTIVE PREPARATION.

"THE MARRIED WOMAN'S MENTOR."

"SERVANTS: HOW TO OBTAIN THEM AND HOW TO MANAGE THEM."

To be published by

MR. THOMAS BURLEIGH.

THE MARRIED MAN'S MENTOR

BY

Lucas Lovibond.

"—*quos irrupta tenet copula.*"
HORACE.

London:
THOMAS BURLEIGH
1899.

BARNICOTT AND PEARCE
PRINTERS.

CONTENTS.

CHAP.		PAGE
1	The Choice of a Wife	1
2	The Honeymoon	28
3	Settling Down	41
4	Friends and Neighbours	55
5	Relations	70
6	Concerning Servants	87
7	The Wife's Purse	105
8	The Green-eyed Monster	127
9	For Richer, for Poorer	142
10	In Sickness and in Health	160
11	The First Baby—and the Last	174
12	The Rift within the Lute	193
13	Darby and Joan	213
14	Second Marriages	225

CHAPTER I.

THE CHOICE OF A WIFE.

The Excellence of Marriage.

It was once wittily observed that a book entitled "How to be happy though Single" would have a large sale. But the difficulty would be to fill it. Of course the unmarried, both men and women, have a certain number of opportunities of being happy by making others happy, but, even when full allowance is made for that, the single life remains, as a rule, curiously narrow and limited, both in its interests and its opportunities, when compared with the married state. Moreover, these interests and opportunities generally grow smaller and fewer in the case of unmarried people as the years roll on, while in the case of married people they increase continually as children and grandchildren come on the scene, each claiming, and giving in return, a continual exchange of affection and tender care.

There may be exceptions here and there, but clearly for the great mass of people the married state is in every way the best. Now it is universally agreed by the wisest authorities that in order to enter the married state a man must first choose a wife. "First catch your hare." One would think at first sight that this ought not to be very difficult, seeing that there are some hundreds of thousands more women than men in most countries. Yet as a matter of experience it is found to be not at all easy. Men who are of an age to marry may be roughly divided into those who live at home with their parents or other relations, and those who are condemned to the comparative solitude of lodgings or chambers. Some men make friends whatever their circumstances may be, but even such universal favourites will find the following pages useful.

The Young Man who lives at Home.

THE young man who lives at home with relations is certain to see a good many ladies of suitable age and circumstances. He has sisters whose dearest friends these ladies are, though of course it is doubtful whether they would consider any of them good enough for their darling brother. Opportunity is the great thing needed, but perhaps this particular Edwin has too much of it, and sees so many possible Angelinas that he is bewildered and hesitates, or else grows critical and cynical. Bicycling, tennis, golf, even croquet, all furnish copious opportunities.

The Young Man who lives in Lodgings.

On the other hand, the poor young man who lives in lonely lodgings enjoys few or none of these delightful chances. Often he hardly sees a woman to talk to, except his landlady or the lodging-house "slavey," from one week to another. What a pity that the opportunities of meeting nice, pleasant, suitable girls cannot be more evenly distributed! However, the young man in lodgings is better off than he used to be, for cycling has enormously widened his chances. There is a sort of freemasonry of the wheel, and a chance acquaintance struck up on the road over a broken tire has often led to a closer friendship, ending in a happy marriage. Cycling clubs, too, are excellent for bringing marriageable young men and maidens together, and there are, of course, numerous religious and philanthropic agencies in which a common interest frequently sets the wedding bells a-ringing.

Beauty as a Test.

But, whether you are a young man living at home, or whether you put up with the doubtful comforts of lodgings, the principles which should guide you in the choice of a wife are, after all, much the same. In the first place many wiseacres will

The Choice of a Wife. 7

warn you against choosing a wife for her beauty. But really it is the most natural thing in the world to do so, and it is not at all foolish so long as it is the right kind of beauty.

The face is an open book on which the general character and nature of the owner are written plain for those who have eyes to read it. Many phrenologists and physiognomists, however, pretend to have such marvellous powers of discovering people's characters from their features and "bumps" that they are apt to be regarded as quacks. And yet there is a good deal of foundation for their so-called science. We all of us in our daily lives are constantly judging people by their faces. Often, no doubt, we make mistakes, but the fact remains that in many cases the face and look and manner are enough to go upon in forming a rough practical opinion of a person.

Novelists are very fond of introducing us to wonderful men who can "read a woman like a book," and can find out her most intimate feelings and emotions from the mere sight of her features. Of course experience of human nature does give one a certain insight into the more common types of mankind, but practically all that can be done with safety is to form quite a general opinion, which you must be ready to revise or modify at any moment. It is a fatal thing to form an impression at first sight, whether favourable or the reverse, and let it run away with you.

Now apply these principles to the choice of a wife, and you will see how they will help you in recognising true beauty. It is the simple truth that good temper, good sense, an affectionate disposition, and all that is implied in the word "goodness," will make a woman look beautiful even if she is not favoured by Nature with ideally perfect features. This is the kind of beauty that lasts.

On the other hand, how often you may see a face which is almost perfectly beautiful in repose, spoiled by the fatal signs of ill-temper, spitefulness, vanity, or stupidity. The worst of these is stupidity, for the other disagreeable qualities may be lessened and even cured, but a lack of ordinary intelligence can never be remedied.

Beware of choosing the companion of your life in the same way that you would choose a partner at a dance. This may seem to some a needless warning, but it is really astonishing how often an otherwise sensible man is attracted to quite the wrong girl for him by the most trivial accidents —a pretty, well-fitting dress, a smart repartee, a curly lock of hair that has strayed out of its place.

The Stupid Woman.

THE stupidest women are the most dangerous to the marrying man, for there is no quality so necessary to a woman in marriage as good sense and intelligence. She will need it from the very moment the marriage ceremony is over. Of course it is a good thing for a single woman to be sensible and intelligent, but her opportunities are so limited by comparison. A married woman, on the other hand, is called upon to exercise these qualities every hour of the day. She must have sense, and tact, and that indefinable power of making things go smoothly, or else she will make both herself and her husband miserable.

Unfortunately it is often the stupid women who are more attractive than their intelligent sisters. Their very stupidity is a kind of subtle flattery to the men they meet. They affect a pretty kind of helplessness, which many men foolishly think charming and feminine. It is all very well, perhaps, for an hour or two at a picnic or a party, but how tiresome for a whole lifetime!

And don't flatter yourself, my dear sir, that you can guide this sort of girl through life by means of your superior wisdom! Talk, explain, lecture till your head aches—what

The Choice of a Wife.

you say only goes in one ear and comes out at the other. The charm of her childishness will soon wear off, but her silliness will always remain, and you will have to bear the consequences of her perpetual blunders in the practical affairs of life. In any crisis, such as illness, when prompt action is all important, she will either sit down and cry and do nothing, or else she will hysterically do just the wrong thing. So, too, with regard to your friends. Instead of being a help to you in your career, she will be always offending people, who might be useful to you, by her tactlessness and stupidity.

In fact, to put it plainly, you cannot afford to marry a girl of this sort, unless indeed you have no ambition, and have already as much money and as good a position as you are ever likely to want. Even if you are so fortunate as that, you would still, remember, have to put up with her silliness all your joint lives. And you would have to be very much in love with her to bear with that—not for a week, nor for a month, but for an indefinite number of years.

Miss "Manager."

HERE is the place to warn you of an opposite danger. Do not, in avoiding the stupid or silly girl, throw yourself

The Choice of a Wife.

into the arms of the woman who goes in for being clever and managing. This kind always thinks she knows better than anyone else. Sometimes she does, but generally she doesn't. She is everlastingly trying to manage other people's business for them. She does not make any charge for her advice, which is perhaps just as well, since it is worth, as a rule, rather less than nothing. Her great mistake lies in treating people as if they were either children or machines. If you give her a chance she will, metaphorically speaking, "smack you and put you to bed," or dispose of you as if you had no more feelings than a footstool. A whole family she will set by the ears, and then wonder why they are so quarrelsome.

You may think, in your innocence, that it would be rather pleasant to be managed and told what to do, and so saved a lot of trouble. Ask her relations what they think. If they are candid, they will say "Better take on the trouble." They know what it is to have a pragmatical person perpetually putting them right, and telling them that their "duty" is this and that. For this kind of woman is generally great on what she calls "duty." She does not understand that a woman's true duty is to be kind and amiable, indulgent to the faults of others, stern to her own, always thinking the best of people, and spreading happiness and contentment round her by the magic gifts of sympathy and tactful good sense.

How to distinguish.

But you will say, "How am I to distinguish between the managing woman who is to be avoided, and the intelligent, sensible woman whom I am, if possible, to marry?" It is a reasonable question enough, for the managing woman often appears, particularly on first acquaintance, to be both intelligent and sensible.

The answer is that you must not rush headlong into a proposal, but must have patience, and keep your eyes and ears open. Sooner or later, and more likely sooner than later, the disagreeable managing woman is bound to betray herself. You must remember that in her own eyes she is perfection, or as near perfection as they make them in this imperfect world, and her powers of management are her greatest pride. She is certain to trot them out for your admiration, and then you can apply a very simple test.

How is she regarded by children and old people? Do they love her or dislike her? You may safely be guided by their instinct. It is in their first and in their second childhood that people most want sympathy and tact and unselfishness, and they seem to know instinctively where to look for them.

The Test of Beauty again.

But there is another test by which you should judge all women, and it brings us back to the point we started from—namely, the test of beauty. Of course it is not so simple as it sounds. You must not necessarily pick out the most beautiful woman you know and propose to her. Every woman starts with certain advantages or disadvantages of looks. What you must do is to consider, in the case of any woman who attracts you, whether

her disposition has increased or diminished her beauty.

Take, for instance, a woman who starts with the advantages of well-formed regular features, a clear, healthy skin, and pretty hair. If she is, by nature, stupid or shrewish, interfering or narrow-minded, it must be written on her face. She will certainly be more beautiful in repose than when she is talking or acting. Of course, if you are lucky enough to have opportunities of seeing her in her home circle, you will be able to glean valuable hints from her behaviour there and the sort of feelings she inspires in those who know her best.

Then, by way of contrast, take the woman who is not favoured by nature as regards looks. Her features are plain, if not absolutely ugly, but if she have sense, intelligence, goodness, tact, amiability, you will think, as she talks to you, that her face is pleasing and even beautiful. Her loyal, true nature will shine out of her honest eyes, and almost everything she says will reveal her sterling character and her freedom from affectation and selfishness. Mentally, you will put her down, in the expressive phrases of the day, as " a real good sort," and as thoroughly " white." Probably it will also occur to you that, as a companion for life, she would wear better than the other type.

You may, of course, be so lucky as to meet a woman whose natural beauty has not spoiled her, but is enhanced by the beauty of her mind and soul and disposition. In that case there is no need to hesitate. Nor is there in the case of the ugly woman whose bad disposition has made her still uglier. She may be safely left alone.

Marrying for Money.

THIS is a very delicate question, and one in which it is almost impossible to lay down any general rules. But you may be certain of one thing, at any rate, that if you marry a woman whom you do not care for, simply and solely for her money, you will bitterly regret it. You will inevitably become a sort of appendage to her—a part of her retinue, like her lap-dog and her pussy-cat. No man who respects himself could be happy in such a position.

On the other hand, it would be foolish, if you are really attached to a girl who is well off, to give up all thought of her because of her money. If she cares for you in the same way, she will never think that the money influenced you. Her relations may be disagreeable, and officious friends may talk, but what will that matter?

But you must be careful not to give up your occupation, whatever it is. Even if the girl has plenty for both, and your salary would only be a trifling addition to the joint income, yet on no account give it up. Independence means happiness, and you would not be independent if you were living as a pensioner on your wife's bounty.

Unfortunately it is often the case that honourable and high-minded men, who would make good husbands, are frightened away from girls who have money, by a Quixotic dislike even to run the risk of the slightest suspicion of fortune hunting; while men of another type, who have an eye simply for money, rush in and bear away the prize. Such marriages are seldom or never successful, and the poor girl finds when it is too late that her money has been to her a curse instead of a blessing.

After all, it is easy to be too particular about the opinion of others. If you are true to yourself, if you are firmly convinced that your happiness is centred in a particular girl, and that you would be as willing to marry her from a cottage as from her comfortable villa or country mansion, then it would be in the last degree foolish to sacrifice both her happiness and yours for the sake of avoiding some problematical gossip. If, however, you cannot honestly say to yourself that the girl's money makes no difference at all, and if you would hesitate for a moment, supposing her to be suddenly deprived of it, then you had far better think no more of her, except as a friend.

True Love.

Last, but not least, a word must be said on the magic power of true love. No observant person of ordinary human sympathies can go through life without realising what a potent factor this is, and yet from its very nature it does not lend itself to definite analysis and description. There are so many imitations of it abroad that it is in danger of being obscured, and it must be admitted that not every person in the world is capable of the unselfish devotion which is its most beautiful characteristic. It lights up and transfigures the prose of every-day life like the glorious sunlight on some ugly city street; it comes unawares like the wind, and defies all efforts to reduce it to rule or to bind it in commonplace fetters. It is impossible to command it, and it may be found in the most unlikely places, but when all has been said of it that can be said, it remains the crown and the truest sanction of married life.

CHAPTER II.

THE HONEYMOON.

Begin as you mean to go on.

THE knot is tied. You have reached the height of your ambition, and are driving away from the wedding breakfast or reception in a cab, the roof of which is covered with old shoes, while the partner of your joys and sorrows is endeavouring to get the rice out of her dress. This is the point at which to impart to you the true secret of a happy married life, namely, Begin as you mean to go on. There can be no severer test of this precept than the honeymoon, especially if you have decided to adopt one of the traditional kind. For the conventional month you will be left quite to yourselves, none of your friends being so indiscreet as to break in upon love's young dream; you will have nothing to do, your wife will not even have any domestic duties, and you will probably be travelling about a good deal.

The Test of Travelling.

Now it is well known that there is no severer test of ordinary friendship than travelling about in company. In that one month you and your wife will have more of one another's society than you are ever likely to have in any succeeding month of your whole married life, and it is obviously all the more necessary that a good start should be made. You two will be as solitary, in a way, as if you had been thrown up on a desert island, the sole survivors of some terrible shipwreck, and the conditions altogether will be so unwonted as to test severely your powers of adaptability and companionship.

Most old married people look back on their honeymoon through rose-coloured spectacles, but it is certain that a goodly number, if they were quite candid, would admit that it was not altogether a time of unalloyed bliss. No human being is perfect, and really the ordinary kind of honeymoon seems as if it had been expressly contrived to bring to light, and even magnify, any little faults of temper, disposition, and so on, which had lain hid throughout the golden hours of courtship. It is, in short, too great a trial for ordinary human nature.

Beware of Boredom.

Unless you are very certain both of yourself and of your wife, you would do well to make the honeymoon shorter than the regulation month, but in any case, even if circumstances render it advisable to make it so long, you should by all means devise some occupation in which both your wife and yourself may be interested. Any taste which you have in common with her, whether it is an out-door exercise, such as cycling or golf, or the pursuit of an art, such as water-colour drawing or photography, will serve the purpose excellently. The great danger against which you must guard is boredom, and if you go away without some preservative against that most fatal destroyer of connubial happiness, you will be doing a very rash thing.

Where to go.

THIS selection of some occupation will also be serviceable in guiding you as to the choice of a place where to spend the honeymoon. The time of the year will of course affect your decision, but if you are married in the spring, as is generally done, you will probably be urged to go to the seaside, or to Devonshire, or to the Lakes. Now, the objection to these resorts is, that you will find them full of newly-married couples already, and it is generally admitted that "honeymooners" do not make the liveliest society in the world. Moreover, do what you will, you will certainly be "spotted" as a honeymoon couple by the hotel keepers and landladies, and though they may feel a certain sentimental interest in your position, it will not be strong enough to induce them to take anything off the bill. Newly-married couples are everywhere recognised as fair game for extortion, and unless you are prepared to pay through the nose, as the saying is, you had better avoid the more obvious holiday resorts.

There is much to be said for choosing a place or district a little out of the beaten track, where the inhabitants are primitive and honest, or where they are accustomed to receive strangers all the year round and are consequently not so extortionate as

The Honeymoon.

the people who depend on one season of the year only for their profits. You want plenty of change of scene and plenty of interest and occupation, and to secure these it is probable that you cannot do better than to go to some foreign country. The great capitals of Europe, such as Paris, Rome, Berlin, and Vienna, are nowadays so accessible, and afford accommodation to suit all purses, that in any of them a cheap and yet most interesting time may be spent. Or, if you do not care for great cities, almost every continental country nowadays welcomes the tourist, even in remote villages and small country towns.

If, however, you prefer to remain

within the limits of the United Kingdom, you will do well to select some district which has a marked individuality, both in its inhabitants and in its scenery, and which is also quite fresh and unexplored to both of you. The remoter parts of Scotland and Wales, the dales of Yorkshire, and the wild coast scenery of Cornwall, immediately suggest themselves, and, with care, should not prove much more expensive than a continental honeymoon.

The Golden Rule.

But wherever you go, and whatever occupation you decide upon together, never forget that golden rule already mentioned, Begin as you mean to go on ; do not have one kind of temper for the honeymoon, and another, less pleasant, for ordinary work-a-day life. There should not, if you have married the right kind of girl, be any question as to which of you is to be master, but as no girls are perfect, it is better to settle any little question of the kind that may arise, rather during the honeymoon than later.

As a matter of fact, in a partnership of mutual aid and companionship, such as marriage, most questions which have to be decided will fall naturally within the province of one or the other partner, as is known to be the case in an ordinary business partnership; the rest, consisting of matters which do not fall obviously within the province of either of you, should be settled amicably in consultation. If, from the very start, you carry out this principle of division of labour, you will have a very much better prospect of a happy married life.

The Need for Imagination.

THERE is no relation of life in which it is more necessary to cultivate a certain faculty of imagination than in marriage. You must accustom yourself to look at things, to a certain extent, from your wife's point of view. Hitherto you have spent your holidays in the society, probably, of some man friend, whose physical powers were pretty well equal with your own; it is, however, rare to find a woman who can, as a regular thing, walk as far as a man, and do as much sight-seeing, and so on.

Many a husband, for want of imagination, has put himself quite wrong with his wife in those early days of married life on which so much depends of after happiness. Of course, it has been the very last thing he intended to make his wife ill, but you cannot too often remember that you are physically stronger than your wife, and it will rest with you, in all probability, to estimate how much going about she can manage with safety, for you may be sure that she will be only too ready to do more than she ought, from a praiseworthy fear of spoiling your enjoyment. Moreover, it is this kind of thoughtfulness which specially endears a man to a woman, and is the surest foundation for long years of happy married life.

CHAPTER III.

SETTLING DOWN.

THE golden days of the honeymoon are over, and you are returning to resume your place in the work-a-day world. Many young couples set up housekeeping at first in apartments, and the plan has a good deal to recommend it, especially if the wife is entirely ignorant of housekeeping. For in apartments, particularly if the landlady is a kind and capable woman, the wife may make her little experiments, and acquire the experience of domestic matters which she lacks, without wasting as much money as she would in a house of her own. Still, the majority of young couples prefer to start their married life under the shelter of their own roof, however humble it may be.

A Trial to your Wife.

Now, my dear sir, you must remember that the process of settling down is likely to be much more of a trial to your wife than to you. You go back to your work, your office in the city, or the active pursuit of your profession, whatever it may be, but she has no such resource. For a con-

Settling Down.

siderable time past she has been accustomed to see a great deal of you. I imagine that during the courtship you spent with her every hour which you possibly could, and naturally you were still more with her during the honeymoon.

But now, from the very moment you and she return home all is changed. As soon as breakfast is over you leave for your work, unless, of course, you are a doctor with a surgery attached to your house, or some other kind of professional man who is not called upon to do his work away from his home. But, in the great majority of cases, the young bridegroom is obliged to leave his wife alone for the greater part of the day.

To keep your Wife Company.

Your natural suggestion will be, I suppose, to get in somebody to keep your wife company while you are away. You will certainly be recommended, before you go away for your honeymoon, to have in some relation to welcome you on your return. Now I do not recommend this plan at all, unless, indeed, both you and your wife are fortunate enough to know of somebody in whom you both feel an extraordinary amount of confidence, and of whom you are both exceptionally fond.

Ordinarily it is not wise to have anyone at all staying in the house just when you are settling down. It is better that your wife should face the trials of housekeeping alone. She will, of course, make mistakes, but she will probably learn more quickly by experience if she is left to fend for herself, with only such assistance as you are able to give her.

The Old Family Servant.

It is a mistake, too, I think, to take on, as many Benedicts do, some old and trusted family servant of theirs to guide the faltering steps of the young wife in the thorny paths of house-wifery. Very often a man will, on his marriage, insist on keeping some servant whom he has found valuable as a bachelor. The result is that the domestic treasure tyrannizes most dreadfully over the poor young wife, who does not like to object to a servant who is so much valued by her husband.

It is better in almost every way to start quite fresh, especially if you, my dear sir, are prepared to treat your wife's beginnings in domestic economy with good-natured indulgence. You may, perhaps, think now and again regretfully of the comfort which the old family servant could bestow on you, but at any rate you ought to take a more than equal pleasure in helping your wife to meet the difficulties which confront her, and which generally seem much greater than they are in reality.

Grumbling.

It is in these early days of married life that some women unconsciously drop into the habit of perpetually grumbling. When the husband returns from work in the evening, tired and perhaps a little cross, he is met by a dismal catalogue of all the domestic troubles which have occurred since he left home in the morning. This habit is one which women fall into very easily, and if there is to be domestic peace and happiness in the home, you must be on the look-out for the first signs of it, and must gently and tactfully turn your wife away from the habit of complaint.

You will best be able to do this by frankly sharing the little troubles of the household with her. "Two heads are better than one" is a good old proverb, and it belongs to the very fundamental idea of marriage that you should assist one another in your several troubles and difficulties. Thus you may accustom your wife from the earliest days of marriage to look persistently on the bright side of things, and to keep a brave heart, even if the maid has given warning, and the water pipes have burst, and a battalion of cockroaches is marching up from the kitchen into the bedrooms!

Plenty to do.

As a matter of fact, you will find that the period of settling down will not be an idle one for either of you. You may at first, when you are working in your office, wonder to yourself what your wife can possibly find to be doing all the long hours of the morning and the afternoon, but practically there will be no lack of occupation and even amusement for her, if she goes about the business in the right way. Even if the house itself is not new, probably the furniture and things in it are all new, and though no doubt they have been arranged and planned already, yet practical experience of them suggests numberless little changes and the addition of many little improvements.

Then again, there will be callers. There will be social duties, for brides are always popular, and a wedding call must be returned without any delay. Moreover, there are many things which you and your wife will have to settle and about which you did not bother yourselves during the delightful, lazy time of courtship. I mean such things as the household budget, with the careful alloting of expenditure on each item in its due proportion.

Beginning to Know One Another.

GENERALLY speaking, the time of settling down is one of great importance to your future happiness. It is then that you and your wife begin really to know one another's natures, and if you on your part strive to keep your best side constantly turned towards her, if you are always kind and gentle and forbearing, though at heart you may feel cross and tired, you will reap the benefit in years to come.

It is from these beginnings of married life that a woman is apt to form a definite judgment of the man with whom she is to spend her life, and if only you begin well in the early days, it will be infinitely easier for you to keep the love and respect of your wife through the years that are to come.

The Tameness of the Domestic Hearth.

IT is probable that as a bachelor you took part with zest in all a young man's amusements, athletics, billiards, and so on, and it may well be that the domestic hearth may seem to you at first somewhat tame. A kind of despair may perhaps strike you when you ask yourself whether you are to spend all your evenings for the rest of your life in reading a book aloud, or playing a game of backgammon, and so you may be tempted, especially if the process of settling down involves a certain amount of domestic discomfort, to leave your wife and return to the club or wherever you formerly met your bachelor associates.

Assuredly they would greet you with enthusiasm, but it is a temptation which you must sternly resist. Your wife stands in particular need of your presence and help when she is starting on her career as a married woman. In after years, perhaps, when she has children to occupy her mind, your occasional absence in pursuit of masculine amusements would not distress her; indeed, she would probably feel glad to think that you were enjoying yourself.

It is different, however, in these early weeks; and, after all, there is no need for you to sit evening after evening, one on each side of the fireplace, like a pair of tabby cats. Fortunately there are many forms of rational entertainment and recreation in this country to which a man may take his wife ; while, when the end of the week comes, many charming little trips to places of interest and beauty in the neighbourhood can be arranged, and thus you will find, I am convinced, that in losing the distractions of bachelorhood you have made a more than proportional gain.

CHAPTER IV.

FRIENDS AND NEIGHBOURS.

It is generally assumed that the effect of marriage is largely destructive of old friendships on both sides, but there is really no reason why this should be the case as a rule, although, to be sure, we can all of us recollect cases within our own knowledge in which marriage has had the result of reducing friendships to the level of mere acquaintanceships.

Bachelor Chums.

INEVITABLY marriage must make a great change in the relations of both the husband and the wife to their own immediate circle. It is often assumed when a man is married that his wife will not be at all pleased if he keeps up the old chums of his bachelor days. If so, it is a pity he married her, for she must be a selfish and ill-conditioned woman to object to her husband's faithfulness to those who esteem him and whom he esteems.

The friends whom a man has made in business are frequently of considerable importance to him, and a wise woman will stretch a good many points, and will even go out of her way to make them feel that they are welcome under her husband's roof. She will even forgive the lingering flavour of cigar smoke in her best curtains, or the soiling of her immaculate doorstep with careless masculine boots.

So, too, with the friends whom you have made, perhaps, in the athletic world; your wife will do well to encourage any taste you may have for cricket, or football, or golf, or cycling, for instance, wherewith the cares of business may be relieved, even though it may deprive her of a certain portion of your society.

Hints for the Husband.

On the other hand, a word may be said to you. It may be that your wife may have a prejudice against some particular friend of your bachelorhood. In such a case it is better, if you can, to conciliate her by gradually reducing him to the position of an acquaintance, or even dropping him altogether. After all, you owe more consideration to your wife's feelings than to your friend's, and there may be more reason in her prejudice than you are yourself aware. This is particularly the case if she has no foolish prejudices against all your friends in general, but only shows hostility to one of them.

Again, a bachelor may have friends who are very good fellows, and in whom there is no particular harm, but who may be nevertheless quite unsuitable for home use. There are not a few confirmed bachelors whose Bohemianism has become so much a second nature that when in an ordinary English household they feel like "a trout in a lime basket," to use Mr. Samuel Weller's simile. If you have friends of this type who shine in the free-and-easy intercourse of bachelor's lodgings or of the social club, but who are out of their depth in a lady's drawing-room, then you must take the bull by the horns and abstain from inviting them to your house. They will, in their secret hearts, be grateful to you, for the sight of your domestic happiness would simply bore them; and on your side you will, by never asking them, avoid certain difficulties and awkwardnesses in the future.

It will be wise to take your wife fully into your confidence with regard to all those friends whom you do invite to the house. Let her understand clearly the feelings you entertain towards each of them, and explain to her which of them you are fond of solely for their own sakes, and which of them you regard in the light of useful business friends.

Here, perhaps, I may say a word

Friends and Neighbours. 61

of warning to older married men who have families of young people round them. There is, of course, much to be said for the freedom which is accorded to English girls, but none the less it behoves the fathers of families to be careful as to the men who visit regularly at the house. Any carelessness in this respect may bring untold misery to innocent lives. Remember, too, that it is a great but unfortunately common mistake to suppose that old men can always be implicitly trusted.

Your Wife's Friends.

Then there is the question of your wife's friends, and of your own joint friends. Do not expect to be very popular yourself with your wife's friends, especially those of the fair sex. If you have chosen your wife in accordance with the principles laid down in the chapter on "The Choice of a Wife," her friends will owe you rather a grudge for taking her away from them, and the more fond they are of her, the less they are likely to be fond of you.

This may sound unreasonable, but it is human nature, and you must endeavour to make your wife feel that in marrying you she has not lost but gained. It is not very likely, if she is the right sort of woman, that she will allow her family friends to make mischief or to set her against you; but, at the same time, she can hardly help being influenced to some extent by people whom she has known for a long time, and it will be only prudent for you to watch the sort of people who visit your wife on the basis of old friendship.

Generally speaking, it is impossible for these old friends to understand that your wife's new duties and new interests must necessarily withdraw her to a great extent from their society, and they will not abate their claims on her without something of a struggle. Allow a certain reasonable period for the struggle. Give them time to find out that they are no longer quite so important to your wife as they were, and if they still insist on seeing more of her than is reasonable, then you and she must together concert a plan for making them aware of the necessary change which your marriage has made. Probably this will not really be necessary, and you will find that they will gradually drop off for the most part, and that in the end your wife will retain just the few intimate family friends whom she really needs.

Neighbours.

A WORD of warning is very necessary with regard to neighbours. You and your wife have probably settled down

Friends and Neighbours.

in a new neighbourhood, and are being called upon by the society of the place. You will do well to remember that it is much easier to make useless and undesirable acquaintances than to shake them off when they are made. Every town and village, and suburb, contains a certain number of idle, rather brainless, people, who have nothing to do but to pay visits, and talk, and gossip from morning till night. Much of this gossip is harmless, but there is always a certain remnant which does mischief, and if you are a professional or a business man it may easily do you real financial injury.

The task of shaking off such people

without an open quarrel must inevitably fall mainly on your wife's shoulders, but if she has tact, and feels perfectly sure of herself, she will manage it without really giving offence. Of course it is not an easy thing to manage, and it is almost impossible to avoid mistakes ; but, on the other hand, when people are really undesirable acquaintances, their reputation generally precedes them, and it ought not to be difficult to ascertain, unobtrusively, the feelings with which any particular family are regarded by those who already know them.

Holiday Companions.

It remains to consider the people who may be described as the joint friends of both you and your wife. As to these there should be no difficulty, for we may assume that they are doubly welcome whenever they come to see you. It is with friends of this kind only that you should ever make up holiday parties. It has already been explained that travelling is the great trial and test of friendship, and if you wish to look back on your holidays with feelings of pleasure, you must be very careful with whom you go. There are many people who settle this question very simply by never going away except by themselves, but most people are more sociable than that, in fact, often too sociable, for they make up parties of individuals who are as likely to mix as oil and water, and disagreements and unpleasantnesses inevitably arise.

A hint in conclusion. If a particular family displays great eagerness to go away with you for a tour or an excursion, and is very anxious for you to settle it on the spot and fix the day, and so on, no doubt it is to some extent a testimony to the charm of your and your wife's society, but do not forget that it may also be due to the inability of this family to get anyone else to go away with them. After all, the people who make the pleasantest travelling companions are generally in great request. It is the dull people who find a difficulty in making their arrangements.

CHAPTER V.

RELATIONS.

It has been said that Adam and Eve started life under ideal conditions because they had nothing to fear from the advice of relations, and certainly there is no doubt that relations sometimes play a most unfortunate part in married life. Of course there are people who deliberately make mischief among all those connected with them, and take a pleasure in doing it. With such people you must deal shortly and sharply. The real difficulty is to manage with relations and intimate friends who make mischief without in the least meaning to do so. They mean it honestly in pure kindness, but that does not, unfortunately, lessen the pain and trouble they cause.

Your Mother=in=Law.

ALTHOUGH it is the correct thing to pity a man for having a mother-in-law and for being more or less surrounded, at any rate during the first few years, or perhaps we should say months, of his married life by his wife's relations, it must be admitted that too often it is the husband's relations who, without being in the least aware of it themselves, overshadow the bridal home.

I think you will find, my dear sir, that your mother-in-law has in her secret heart a wholesome fear of you. She knows only too well, poor soul, the sort of stories that are told about the interference of the wife's mother, and in any domestic difference you will find, perhaps with some astonishment, that she will generally take your part. A considerable knowledge and experience of married life will have taught her that submission is, from the wife's point of view, often the best policy, and the fonder she is of her daughter the more anxious she will be to keep on good terms with that daughter's husband.

When people speak of the part relations play in married life they genally concentrate all their sarcasms on mothers-in-law, but it by no means follows that other relations may not unwittingly play quite as disagreeable a part.

Your own Mother.

Your own mother, of course, considers you almost if not quite perfection. However fond she may be of your wife, you may be quite sure that she does not consider her exactly good enough for you. Now it very rarely happens that a man in any country, except France, chooses his bride exactly in accordance with his parents' wishes and plans, and so your mother is sure to think that your young wife has a great deal to learn. She would like to see this novice in housekeeping profit by her long experience, for above all things she naturally wishes to see you made as comfortable in your new home as you were under your father's roof. The one woman in the world to whom a man ought never to complain of his own wife is his mother, and it may almost be said in the same breath that the one woman whom a husband should never quote to his wife is her mother-in-law.

Sisters and Sisters-in-Law.

SISTERS, whether they belong by blood to you or to your wife, may wreck your happiness quite as surely as your mother-in-law or your own mother, and quite as unconsciously. Too often a man's married sister constitutes herself his wife's guide, philosopher, and friend. She is determined to see her brother's home managed exactly like her own, and she generally imagines that a few years of married life have given her a vast amount of experience which she is anxious to pass on to her new "sister." In the nature of things she cannot really have the same anxiety as to the happiness and welfare of the young couple as even the most stern of mothers-in-law must have.

Accordingly, beware of allowing your sister or your sister-in-law to gain too firm a footing in your household. Often a young man sees the pleasanter side of life at a married sister's ; he admires the way she manages her house and her husband, and he does not realize that, when all is said and done, he is only introduced—if she is a wise woman—to the bright side of her establishment.

Beware of Gossip.

It would be quite impossible to overestimate the amount of harm which is done in families by the talk, or rather gossip, which goes on among near relations. Too often the husband's brothers, sisters, father, and mother, seem to take quite a cruel delight in talking over the bride and telling each other all about her mistakes and failures. This is notably the case when the first baby appears on the scene. Then every matron in the immediate circle has her say, especially those who are old enough to have forgotten how they brought up their infants; and unless the whole family are exceptionally high-minded and kindly, not only are the wildest accusations bandied to and fro, but too often some candid friend repeats what has been said, perhaps half in joke, to the young wife, who, though she probably says nothing, is thereby permanently set against her husband's people.

Don't let your Wife be Discussed.

SET your face firmly against all discussion of your wife, even though it be done in the very kindest manner, by your own old home circle. After all, her success or failure as a housekeeper, as a mother, and as a woman of the world, is your business, not that of your relations, unless, indeed, you have made the fatal mistake of setting up housekeeping in common with your parents, or with a brother or sister.

The real reason why joint house-keeping plans generally succeed in France is because French people are trained from early childhood never to say anything disagreeable, either to, or of, their near relations. The sort of perpetual criticism which goes on in the United Kingdom is quite unknown there. Moreover, the various members of a household live very separate lives ; the bed-sitting-room is the rule and not the exception ; and the various members of the household rarely meet excepting at meals. This sort of plan would not suit British sentiment at all, accordingly it is very much better that each household should be formed on quite a separate plan, and stand, as it were, four-square to the world.

Your Wife's Relations.

WHILE on the delicate subject of relations, it may be as well to give you a hint which you will find will go far to sweeten married life. Do not give way to the temptation, or pleasure, of criticising and discussing in an unfavourable sense your wife's relations to herself. Even if she assents to what you say, it will give her pain and perhaps hurt her more than you are at all aware. All the world knows that, while the wife may occasionally speak ill of her husband, she will be exceedingly angry if she hears anyone else attack him. Similarly, although your wife may complain to you that her brother is extravagant or that her sister is a flirt, she will not enjoy hearing the same home-truths from you—indeed, she will probably be grateful to you in the long run if you rebuff her assertions with some kindly and good-natured word.

This is, of course, specially true when you are discussing your father-in-law and mother-in-law. Of them you should never speak ill to your wife. You must remember that to her they stand in an intensely near and intimate relation, though to you they are, after all is said and done, very little more than strangers, with whom fate has thrown you into close and perhaps not altogether delightful proximity. Woe betide you if you repeat to your wife anything unpleasant said of her relations by any of your friends! She will bear a grudge against the unlucky man who observed that "he did not think your little sister-in-law as pretty as other people thought her," or who declared that "your father-in-law's wine was always corked," long after both you and he have completely forgotten the incident.

A Hint on Hospitality.

NEVER be beguiled into offering hospitality, for any length of time be it understood, to a brother-in-law or sister-in-law, unless they are of an age to fend for themselves. It sounds very inhospitable, but, nevertheless, I would earnestly implore you never to take any responsibility of the kind on your own shoulders. You will be held answerable if anything goes wrong, while all the time you have no real authority over the young person in question. It is by no means easy to have charge of a young man, or of a girl only slightly younger than oneself, and when the charge is complicated by near relationship, the result is apt to be disastrous to mutual good-feeling and even to respect.

Step=Relationship.

It is, perhaps, not generally recognised how common step-relationship is in its various degrees. Look round you, and you will be astonished to see how many of these step-relationships exist in every circle. It may be your lot to marry a girl who has been brought up by a step-mother, or whose family circle has consisted mostly of a number of step-brothers and step-sisters. When dealing with this state of affairs it certainly behoves you to walk warily, and to remember that, after all, your first and foremost duty is to your wife. You are bound to take her part whatever may betide. But it need hardly be said that neither you nor she really owe so great a duty to step-relations as you do to each other's full relations in blood.

A Concluding Hint.

PERHAPS it may help you in solving the problem of dealing with relations in general, if you remember how easily you may some day stand in the same relationship to others that others now stand in to you. Thus, it might be well for you occasionally to remind both your wife and yourself that if you each live long enough, she will almost certainly some day be a mother-in-law herself, and you will be a father-in-law. Seriously, relations are not by any means the easiest problem of married life. While treating them all with kindness and courtesy, do not be too ready to admit them to the intimacy of your home—at least not until you have to some extent tested their characters and seen whether the metal rings true.

CHAPTER VI.

CONCERNING SERVANTS.

THE servant question is always with us, and has both its amusing and its tragic side, as readers of the comic papers are well aware. It is to be feared that most house-wives are brought by circumstances to see the tragic more clearly than the comic side, and there is a great deal to be said in favour of the poor lady who declared that she would rather have two serpents in her house than one extra servant. Wherever two or three ladies are gathered together, especially over the teacups, the conversation is pretty sure to come round sooner or later to the engrossing subject of servants; and the fact that children, with their imitative instincts, are passionately fond of playing at being the distracted mistress of a household of bad domestics, shows how much they pick up on this subject from their elders.

"None of my Business."

In all the discussions on the servant question it always seems to be assumed that the matter is one solely for the wife to manage. The burden of it is regarded as falling entirely on her shoulders, while the privilege of grumbling is reserved for the husband. You will be well advised, my dear sir, if you depart from tradition in this respect. Do not say, "It is none of my business!" It is your business, and it is eminently a business in which a little judicious interference on your part will go a very long way to lessen the worry of domestic management for your wife, and to make the wheels of the household machine run smoother. From the lowest point of view, it pays the master of the house to take an intelligent interest in the servant question, and not simply to expect good service to be supplied, laid on, like water or gas.

You must remember that in the class from which servants are mostly drawn, the position of the master of the house is more supreme than in the classes above them. The artisan and the labourer is, as a rule, more the autocrat of his cottage than the most despotic Oriental potentate, and the whole domestic machine revolves round him and the requirements of his work and his play. Naturally, his daughters grow up to think that that is the case everywhere. Hence it is that a word from you will go much further with the average servant than a great many words from your wife.

Concerning Servants.

Scolding servants is seldom of much use, though, of course, it is sometimes the only weapon left, short of dismissal. Servants are very like children, except that they are not so willing to learn as many children are. Though it is often denied, I am convinced that in most cases a policy of kindness, mingled with firmness, is the best to pursue. It may not at first appear to be successful, but if it fails in the end, after persistent trial, then the servant who refuses to yield to it must be altogether an exception. Nagging is the one thing that no good servant can endure. Of course, it is a great temptation to relieve one's feelings by scolding, but remember that words of rebuke are much more effective if they are rare and reserved for important matters. It is a fatal mistake to get angry over little trifles, which demand only good-humoured remonstrance.

The "General."

IN some ways the servant problem is easier when only one is kept, and that is the case with the great majority of households, and is tending to become even more usual owing to the multiplication of flats. The economy of one servant is, of course, considerable, for it is well known that for some mysterious reason two servants eat much more than twice as much as one, and do not do twice as much work.

The Inexperienced Young Matron.

MUCH has been written by unpractical champions of servants as to the supposed unkindness and thoughtlessness of mistresses. There may be some truth in this in the case of middle-aged or elderly women, who, soured by considerable experience, are perhaps sometimes apt to be harsh to their domestics. But in the case of young married women it is generally all the other way. They are, if anything, too kind, too good-natured, and too inexperienced. In their anxiety to save the master of the house any disagreeableness, they are too apt to give way in every point to the tyrant in the kitchen, who naturally enough sees how the land lies and takes advantage of the situation.

Do not, then, allow your wife to be imposed upon in this way. Let it be your business to enquire of her as to the arrangements which she is making with the maid, and you and she together in consultation will be able without difficulty to arrive at some practical arrangement which will be fair to both mistress and servant. Above all, be careful never to take the part of the servant in any matter against your wife. That is always a mistake. It may be that in your heart you think your wife is wrong and the servant is right, but you should never say so. It is better to advise her to dismiss the servant with whom she cannot get on and obtain another.

The Household "Treasure."

OF all varieties of the *genus* servant, this is in some ways the most dangerous. She knows she is a treasure. You can see it in every line of her self-satisfied countenance, and in her manner, with its odd mixture of uneasy deference and presumption. Very likely she has held out against wearing a cap, and has successfully carried her point. In many little ways, every day, she will reveal her strong feeling that she is perfectly indispensable; that you cannot possibly do without her; and that, if anything should happen to her, you and your family would collapse like a house of cards. Originally a fairly good servant, and still probably in many ways of superior intelligence to the average run of servants, she has become the tyrant of the household, and regards herself as conferring a considerable favour on the establishment by condescending to belong to it at all. Servants of this type sometimes refuse to go altogether even when they are plainly dismissed. It is impossible for them to conceive that their room might be preferable to their company.

Of course, the problem in the case of any servant who at all resembles this picture must be solved by weighing the comparative advantages and disadvantages of keeping her. If she is an extraordinarily good cook, and both you and your wife are fond of your meals, then it will probably be worth while to put up with a good deal in other ways. Remember that you cannot expect perfection, nor is the average general servant usually found to be a first-rate cook, a first-rate parlourmaid, an experienced butler, and good child's nurse rolled into one. Indeed, if such a prodigy exists, she would be more likely to grace the British Museum than your domestic hearth, unless, to be sure, you should chance to meet her before your marriage and make her the mistress of your household instead of the servant.

The household treasure type of servant is really dangerous because she grows upon you. I mean that, gradually, and perhaps without herself knowing it, your wife gets to think that something dreadful would happen if this fairly good servant were to leave. The moment you see that sort of legend growing up round the servant, you should do your best to counteract it while there is yet time, unless, of course, you should happen to agree with your wife in her opinion of the treasure.

Domestic Experiments.

A WORD of warning is necessary before you start out on the delicate task of investigating your kitchen arrangements. When there is only one servant in a household, the first thing that will occur to any intelligent observer is the desirability of saving labour wherever possible. Your first idea will, no doubt, be to introduce several kinds of labour-saving appliances, which you fondly hope will oil the wheels of the domestic machine.

Do not be too sure of this. Servants are very conservative; they have not a particularly wide intelligence, and it is more difficult for them to adapt themselves to new conditions than you probably can even imagine. Nothing else can explain the persistent attachment of the English cook to the practice of frying steaks, for instance, instead of grilling them You will probably find that your servant has been taught whatever she knows about her work by her mother, or aunt, or a former mistress, whose ideas she regards as the sum of all domestic wisdom. You will have a tough struggle to get her to change any of them, and very likely, unless you are careful, it will end in her giving warning, and then you will taste the joys of the domestic *interregnum* under the superintendence of the British charwoman.

Judicious Flattery.

A GREAT deal may be done by a show of consulting your Abigail as to any little improvements you may desire to introduce. Servants are generally very susceptible to flattery, and it gives them keen pleasure to feel that their opinion is valued and their experience regarded as worth consulting. So, with tact, combined with that mysterious sanctity which, as already explained, surrounds the master of the house in the servant's eyes, you may be able to induce her to carry out your ideas largely under the impression that they are her own.

Servants are not Machines.

THIS brings us to an important principle in the management of servants. Their personal dispositions should be studied, and, though it may seem cynical to say so, their prejudices should be utilized and played upon, as a skilful musician plays upon his instrument, with complete mastery. Every failure to get cheerful and competent service arises, in the great majority of cases, from a persistent habit which people have of treating servants as if they were mere machines. The well-drilled, highly-trained servants of great houses do resemble machines from the point of view of their employers. But the average general servant is different from this. She is not well trained, and she is in need of a certain human sympathy and companionship which the servants in great houses are numerous enough to afford to one another.

Of course, it is fatal to fall into the opposite extreme of too much familiarity with the servant, who, if she is treated in that way, will very likely develop into a full-blown specimen of the household "treasure." You and your wife will find it best to steer a middle course, treating your servant neither as a machine nor as a poor relation, but as a being for whose welfare you are, in part at any rate, responsible, and to whom you have not done all your duty when you have paid her her wages on the right day.

CHAPTER VII.

THE WIFE'S PURSE.

Solomon, no doubt, had other things in his mind when he said that "Money is the root of all evil," but in these days the proverb applies to the wife's purse perhaps more than to anything else. In many households, in fact it may truly be said in the majority of households, more quarrels take place over the spending, and in some cases the saving, of money than about any other mortal thing.

It must be admitted that too often an otherwise happy wife's life is hopelessly embittered by the perpetual effort, not so much to make both ends meet, as to make her husband believe that she is neither a niggard nor a spendthrift.

The Battlefield of Marriage.

ROBERT LOUIS STEVENSON once said that "marriage is not a bed of roses, but a battlefield," and it is sad to think that so many of the battles take place over the £ s. d. question. In every rank of life the wife's purse becomes a vexed question all too soon after marriage, and there is nothing on which even very sensible and good people differ more widely. One will say: "the man who has a wife worthy of the name, and who puts her on a fixed allowance, is, I think, clearly condemned." Another, and in this case a husband, declares, "I cannot understand how men can be so foolish as not to allow their wives a little pocket-money in addition to the regular weekly allowance for housekeeping," while a wife declares that "one of the most frightful mistakes men make now-a-days, is in thinking that the most economical way of keeping house is also to keep the money."

Can Women Manage Money?

The man who holds the point of view that women are unfitted to manage money, and therefore should be trusted with as little of it as possible, may be gently reminded that in the lower working classes, the woman almost invariably has the spending and the apportioning of the wages earned by her husband. Indeed, among the labouring classes it is an axiom that the man who does not hand his wages over to his wife on the Saturday night, is on the highroad to becoming a drunkard. It is the woman who pays over the club money, and the burial insurance, and the rent ; in fact the entire money and business side of life is left in her charge, and, on the whole, she manages wonderfully well. The man, although he actually earns the money in a far more real sense than those husbands do, for instance, who derive an appreciable portion of their income from invested property, is quite content to accept the small sum which must perforce constitute his pocket-money from his wife's hands.

Generosity v. Meanness.

WHEN a marriage or engagement is under discussion, one hears it said too often that " he may be rather extravagant in his ideas, but she has always been such a careful girl that she will restrain him;" or on the other hand, "she is very careless about money, but he is such a good man of business that he will see she does not outrun the constable." For my part I should prefer to hear of a union between two people who were both near and saving in disposition, or again of a marriage where both the man and the girl were noted for their generosity as regards money. To those gifted with any imagination it is difficult to imagine a more miserable state of things than that which must exist between two persons who do not see eye to eye on the important money question. It is a melancholy fact that in such cases the one, and generally it will be the more reckless and generous nature, will soon learn heartily to despise the other, and often with very little reason.

Presents and Charity.

TAKE the two somewhat similar matters of gift-giving and of charity. We are all familiar with the type of man and woman—generally, it must be admitted, of woman—who will spend the lowest possible sum on a wedding present. If her husband, in a rash moment, allows her to choose the present which is to be given as their joint offering to one of his old chums, she will bring back some gaudy trifle, costing a few shillings, where he, perhaps, was prepared to spend as many pounds. It is almost impossible to persuade some people that it is far better to give no present at all, than to give one which has obviously been chosen on account of its extremely small cost. This, of course, does not apply when the givers are not in a position to spend much, but even then there is all the difference between a present chosen with care and forethought, and one which has been picked up solely with a view to making a show at the smallest possible cost.

It is rather a melancholy thing for human nature that husbands and wives are more likely to quarrel over their respective notions of social generosity than they are over the deeper question of charity. Even here, however, it too often happens that quite rich people will take almost any amount of trouble, and, what is more serious, impose any amount of trouble on their friends, rather than put their hands in their pockets and pay out a dole of so many shillings, or so many pounds, in order to help a deserving case. Too often, where the man's instinct would be to send a highly acceptable cheque, the woman will either offer something in kind which has become useless to herself but which she hopes may be useful to the applicant, or, what is in some cases worse, she will try to work off the case on to some friend who is better-hearted than herself.

In this connexion it must, however, be admitted that the wife has probably from early childhood been always taught how very important it is to save money, while schoolboys, especially public-school boys, have generally a fixed and pretty liberal allowance of pocket-money. I do not know why it is, but certainly most parents, especially mothers, keep their girls very much shorter of cash than their boys, and I suppose that is why the feminine mind seems instinctively to consider cheapness as the greatest consideration of all. This is particularly unfortunate when the girls grow up and marry and have to manage a household. Then they find by bitter experience what any business man would tell them at once, that cheapness seldom spells economy in the long run, and, indeed, is often much dearer in the end.

Tradespeople and the Domestic Budget.

IF you, my dear sir, find that your wife has not been trained to a right use of money, and to have what may be called a good buying judgment from childhood, you must not sit down and bewail your miserable fate, or exercise your masculine prerogative of grumbling. If you do that you will only make matters worse by discouraging your wife and rendering her unhappy and desperate of any improvement.

No. What you must do is to go into the whole domestic budget with her, and see how much there is to spend every week, and what proportion of the whole sum can be afforded for each item, such as meat, bread, fish, vegetables, milk, and so on. With your aid and support she will be emboldened to do battle with her tradespeople, who, if they know that you keep an eye on things, will think twice before taking advantage, even in a legitimate way, of her inexperience.

While I am on the subject of tradespeople, let me urge you to run no long credit bills, but to pay up weekly, and to insist upon doing so. If your credit is satisfactory, and you are known in the neighbourhood as a "warm," substantial citizen, you will find that the tradesmen will prefer that you should not pay weekly. But no other system enables you to maintain a sufficient check on the household expenditure, and therefore you should keep a firm upper lip, and resolutely insist on the accounts being rendered as you wish.

The Question of Stores.

WHETHER you live in town or country, the question will certainly be raised whether you should deal at one of the gigantic modern co-operative stores, or with the regular tradespeople of the neighbourhood. In settling this question you will, of course, be guided mainly by the individual preferences of yourself and your wife. But it will be useful to you to remember that these great stores have their disadvantages.

For one thing, it takes a practised and experienced housekeeper to cope with them successfully. They are extremely independent, and they sel-

The Wife's Purse.

dom trouble to consider the individual tastes and prejudices of a single family, whose custom, after all, does not much matter to them. But an ordinary tradesman, though he may not have so extensive a choice of goods to offer, will, if he is a wise man, make himself of the greatest assistance to a young and comparatively inexperienced wife. He will assuredly regard your custom as worth having, and so he will take pains to keep it.

It will certainly, as a rule, be much pleasanter to your wife to deal with respectable and respectful tradespeople, rather than with a great corporation, which, as the phrase goes, has "neither soul to be saved nor body to be kicked," and the employés of which are frequently very uncivil.

I speak from a considerable knowledge of stores. They are none of them satisfactory all round—at least, none that I have ever dealt with. This is especially true in the case of perishable goods, such as meat, fish, and vegetables. One stores sells provisions of excellent quality, but never sends them in time to be cooked for the midday meal. Another will send the things in ample time, but the quality will be more than dubious, and the "English" meat will be English only if Australia be regarded as a part of England. All this involves constant battles and endless correspondence.

Doubtful Economy.

But it will be said that stores must surely be cheaper than ordinary shops, because they buy their goods in such wholesale quantities, and are content with small profits and quick returns. Well, perhaps that was true when stores were first invented, but matters are now much more even. Consider that these big stores almost always pay large dividends to their shareholders, and where do they get the money from if not from their customers? Indeed, for certain articles stores are actually dearer than ordinary tradespeople.

Besides, I am convinced that the rage for cheapness may be carried too far. You may, perhaps, have noticed in the official advertisements of Government contracts that the saving clause, "The Government does not bind itself to accept the lowest or any tender," is always added at the end. The Government knows what it is about. It knows that the lowest tender probably means scamped work and "slop-stuff." It is easy enough to find cheap goods on the one hand, and goods of really excellent quality on the other. The difficulty is to hit the happy medium between stinginess and waste.

Let your Wife have Money to Manage.

You naturally wish your wife to hit that happy medium. Now, to do so she needs experience, and if she is to acquire that experience in its full measure, she must have the handling of money. Of course, she will make mistakes, especially at first, but you must be patient with her and treat such accidents good-humouredly, even though they should involve a little pinching for a week or two. You can regard the money as an investment, to be repaid by the profits of your wife's increased experience. It may be useful, too, for you to reflect that probably you yourself have not always been above reproach in your business transactions, particularly at first.

So you will do well to accustom your wife to the management of money. Let her have a banking account of her own, never mind how small. In these days of keen competition among banks quite small accounts are willingly undertaken.

There is another reason, too, why you should cultivate your wife's business instincts, though it is not a reason which will be very pleasant to you to contemplate—I mean the contingency of your premature death. Nothing is more sad in its way than the position of a woman, verging, perhaps, towards middle age, who has always led a sheltered life without knowing anything of business, and who suddenly finds herself, owing to the death of her husband, dependent in business matters on the good offices of strangers, or, perhaps, not too kindly relations. You certainly ought to do all in your power to guard your wife from such a fate. Moreover, it is not much good insuring your life for her benefit if she remains utterly incapable of administering the money to the best advantage when it falls in.

I know many people have a fixed idea that women are naturally and fundamentally unbusinesslike. To be sure there are a certain number of women who are as helpless as babies in all practical matters, but I hope you, my dear sir, will not have married a woman of that kind; and on the other hand there are plenty of women who have proved conclusively that they possess real business ability, which only needs fostering.

CHAPTER VIII.

THE GREEN-EYED MONSTER.

There is nothing more comic to the outside spectator than jealousy, and yet there is hardly anything more tragic to those who feel and suffer from it. Indeed, it is really no matter for laughter, and it is to be feared that there is no more potent destroyer of connubial happiness.

The Wife's Jealousy.

In this country it is more usually the woman who is jealous of her husband.

In such a case the advice which is ordinarily given to the husband, is, in general terms, that he should not take any notice of the matter; that it is a passing craze of his wife's; and that, if he keeps cool, it will all come right. Sometimes, no doubt, this is so; some trivial incident opens the wife's eyes, and she realises that she has been mistaken; but, unfortunately, in most cases the green-eyed monster is not dismissed so easily.

Often the wife is jealous of her husband's relations, and this is a particularly difficult case to deal with. In such circumstances you must endeavour to soothe your wife's feelings by seeing as little of your relations as you can consistently with your duty to them.

If your wife's jealousy is of the wholesale kind, if she is jealous of everybody with whom you come into contact, whether they are women or men, then it is perhaps better for you to have a clear explanation. You should try, patiently and kindly, to make her see that her attitude is unreasonable; that she cannot expect to live with you as Friday lived with Robinson Crusoe on the desert island; and that in short, though your first duty is to her, still your marriage did not absolve you from your other duties to your relations, your business or your profession, and your friends.

Turning the Tables.

You will probably be able to turn her arguments against herself by asking her what she would feel if you, on your side, were to keep her locked up in a kind of Turkish harem, and were to forbid her to see any friend or acquaintance from day to day. In these explanations you must be very gentle and careful not to wound her feelings unnecessarily, for if you think of it, her jealousy, though excessively inconvenient to you, is really a very great compliment and testimony to the violence of her attachment.

It must be admitted, however, that reason and logic and argument are

The Green-eyed Monster.

very weak weapons against the passion of jealousy, and if they fail, as they are, perhaps, only too likely to fail, then you will be well advised to seek some method of convincing your wife of your real attachment to her, for if she is once convinced of that, the root of jealousy is cut. How you are to convince her depends on many circumstances. For example, if it is possible for you to take a holiday at the time, you will do well to carry her off with you to some quiet spot where, with kind and patient treatment, her feelings may recover their balance.

If everything else fails, you will probably have to try the effect of a temporary separation, but you must be careful to manage it without giving rise to gossip or scandal.

A Supposed Rival.

MORE easy to deal with, perhaps, is the case when the wife is jealous of some particular woman, who is often an employée of her husband in his business, or someone with whom he is associated in religious or philanthropic work. In that case it is your duty to cast aside any foolish feeling of pride and prove the groundlessness of your wife's jealousy by dismissing the employée, or abandoning the perfectly harmless relations which have subsisted between you and the other woman, whoever she is.

After all, you must remember that your wife may have sharper eyes than you, and that she may be aware of the gossip of censorious tongues which are always ready to put the worst possible construction on the most innocent relationships. Moreover, if it is an employee that she is jealous of, you must remember that she is not likely to be jealous of an unattractive or elderly woman.

To Professional Men.

THE most difficult case occurs to professional men. If you are a lawyer, and your wife is jealous of some fair client who consults you, as she thinks, with unnecessary frequency; or if you are a doctor, and your wife is jealous of some fair patient whose constant ailments your wife regards as inconsistent with her look of blooming health; then you are indeed to be pitied, for you can hardly go to your client or patient and say, "I cannot see you any more." I recollect hearing such a case discussed by a famous Q.C., who remarked that he saw nothing for it but for the husband to choose between his profession and his wife, and added that the most satisfactory way of deciding was to spin a coin. Of course, this advice is much too cynical, but it shows, at any rate, that one very shrewd man of the world found the problem more than he could solve.

Perhaps in this case, also, a temporary separation, if managed without open scandal, may be tried as a possible remedy. Otherwise I do not see anything for it but for you to choose your wife in preference to your patient or your client. Without exactly dismissing the latter from your consulting-room or from your office, you must bring the matter on which she is consulting you to as speedy an end as possible. Thus, if you are a doctor, you can send her on to a brother physician whose advice you may modestly affect to regard as more valuable than yours; or if you are a lawyer you may legitimately edge her and her business off into the charge of your partner, if you have one, or at any rate, your confidential clerk.

The Husband's Jealousy.

THERE remains the even more difficult case when it is the husband who is jealous of his wife. Here, too, the usual advice which the man receives is not to take any notice and leave the matter to cure itself by time. But I take leave to think that this is bad advice, for of all the passions which assail the human heart there is none that rankles more deeply than jealousy, and there is none which is so little likely to be cured by the lapse of time.

Another kind of advice which is often given, especially by rather cynical men of the world, is that the husband should set up a counter-irritant, should, in fact, single out some other lady for special attention in order that he may bring his wife to his side again. But this is extremely unfair to the lady who is thus singled out, and also extremely dangerous from the husband's point of view. For it is quite possible that his action may have exactly the opposite effect on his wife to that which he intends. She may regard his seeking consolation elsewhere as an implied sanction of her proceedings, and so what might have remained an unfortunate but passing fancy may develope on her part into a serious passion.

Equally dangerous in its way is, I think, the attitude of complete indifference which is sometimes recommended. This may well pique a high-spirited woman, and drive her to follies from which in her calm senses she would shrink.

The Choice of a Peacemaker.

THE situation is one of those few in life which call for the interposition of some wise and elderly or middle-aged friend. If you, my dear sir, feel no doubt that your wife is beginning to form an undesirable attachment in any quarter, you must be very careful to avoid—I do not say confiding in your own relations, but even allowing them to suspect for a moment that anything is wrong. The interposition must emphatically not come from the side of your family; it must come from her family. You must confide your troubles best of all to your wife's mother, if she is living, or to some really discreet and old relative or very intimate friend of hers.

It is probable that, if you are quite candid with yourself, you will not be able to acquit yourself of all blame in the matter; if you had been as attentive and as affectionate to your wife as you ought to have been, it is hardly possible to imagine there being any necessity for the interposition of a third person. So, if the interposition is successful, you will be able, by behaving differently to your wife in future, to smooth over the domestic trouble and prevent its ever recurring. Many young wives are treated somewhat unfairly, especially if their husbands are much immersed in business, by being left lonely and miserable for quite long periods together; this is the cause, I am persuaded, of many a matrimonial failure.

Letters.

A word must be said in conclusion as to the undesirability of husband and wife opening one another's letters. The perfect trust and confidence which should be the rule between husband and wife make it particularly necessary to insist on this point. It is terrible for a man's friends to feel that they cannot write to him about delicate matters of business, or for his relations to feel that they must weigh every word they write to him lest it should offend his wife. Without the slightest question of wrong-doing of any kind, both husband and wife ought to be left perfectly free in their correspondence.

CHAPTER IX.

FOR RICHER FOR POORER.

It may seem a paradox, but it is, I believe, perfectly true that sudden wealth is really a greater test of matrimonial happiness than sudden poverty.

Wealth as a Trial.

I would not on any account echo the old familiar cant that wealth is an evil, that it is bad to be rich, and that poor people are happier than those who have great possessions. I do not think that is true on the whole, for, though rich people are often discontented, it is not so much their wealth which makes them so, as the fact that they expect too much from their wealth, and are therefore disappointed.

The great reason why wealth is desirable is that it saves its possessors from all the little worries of life, which gradually wear away the spirit and the energy of those who have to undergo them. If you, my dear sir, should be so fortunate as to acquire wealth rapidly, as I am sure I hope you will, you will find it a great trial in many ways, but if you pass successfully through the ordeal, you will certainly find that on the whole your good fortune has added materially to your happiness and to that of your wife. The great thing necessary is to keep a cool head and not to be uplifted with pride at your good fortune.

A Sad Case.

I KNOW of one case, at least, in which a couple, who were devotedly attached to one another so long as they remained in an obscure position, drifted apart almost as soon as the man began to make really large sums of money, and by the time he was able to call himself a millionaire, which happened very soon, he and his wife were, to use an expressive phrase, absolutely "two people."

It is to be feared that in their case the husband was secretly rather ashamed of his wife. He had married her when they were both poor and humble, and naturally, when his wealth opened up for them a higher grade of society, he began to compare her, not to her advantage, with the other women whom he met. It was unfair in the last degree that he should have done so, for, of course, he could not expect her to have the same sort of accomplishments and graces which characterise the women of the leisured classes. No doubt, for women are quick to notice these things, she detected his disillusionment, and hence they drifted more and more apart, while, of course, outwardly preserving the appearance of affection to the world.

Do not, my dear sir, commit the mistake which these good people made. If an angel from heaven had come to them and said, "Don't get rich; don't take the money; it will be to you a curse instead of a blessing!" I fancy that they would have disbelieved the angel, and would have taken the money all the same. Yet it is true on the whole that their money has been to them a curse; that they would have been happier if they had remained in their comparatively humble station ; and that they must now in their secret hearts often think with regret of the time when they were really united. A fine house, plenty of servants, and the contemptuous patronage of well-born persons are poor substitutes for the confidence and conjugal affection which they have lost.

A Sudden Accession of Fortune.

If great wealth should come your way at all suddenly, do not immediately alter your mode of life; do not rush to a house-agent and take the first showy residence on his books which he can palm off on you; do not buy horses and carriages and engage a great retinue of servants all in a hurry. If you do, you will be "done" right and left. An establishment suitable to your new prosperity is not set up all in a moment, and people who are both honest and capable of filling responsible positions in such an establishment take some looking for.

You will find plenty of flatterers and people anxious to make something out of you as a reward for showing you how to spend your money. Keep these at a distance, for they will only bring misery, and you will earn thereby, if not their liking, at any rate their respect. Prefer the old friends who liked you for your own sake before your great prosperity, and make it your business to benefit them out of your superfluity.

Above all, see that your wife gets advantages from your wealth. Let her, if she has not one already, have a banking account of her own, and furnish it with enough for her to feel that she can benefit some deserving case or help a friend without necessarily troubling you to draw a cheque.

Queen Victoria's Example.

I OFTEN think that the Queen sets the best example to her subjects, and indeed to the world in general, of the wise expenditure of large sums of money, and of the wise management of great establishments. When she came to the throne the waste and extravagance which prevailed in the Royal palaces would hardly be credited nowadays, and much of Prince Albert's early unpopularity was due, it is to be feared, to the energy with which, at the Queen's desire, he set to work to reform these abuses. He succeeded, and ever since the Royal households have been managed on principles which are liberal without ostentation and economical without meanness.

In another respect, too, I think the Queen's example is worth following, namely, in her independence with re-

For Richer for Poorer. 151

gard to matters of taste. I have no doubt, for instance, that her art collections contain much that the superfine critics of the day would condemn as "rubbish," and much also that they would greatly admire. But the Queen does not care. Her pictures and statues and furniture are what please her, and she has the courage of her opinions.

Pictures and Furniture.

IF great wealth falls to your lot, I advise you and your wife to have the courage of your opinions also. Money can do most things nowadays, and you would find plenty of people only too ready to equip you with complete collections of dubious Old Masters, alleged Queen Anne furniture, and Wardour Street *bric-à-brac*. But a man looks simply ridiculous as the owner of possessions which represent other people's taste, not his own. You do not want to be laughed at behind your back, and so let your surroundings be the honest and genuine expression of your own and your wife's preferences.

Comfort should be the first consideration, both in choosing a house and in furnishing it. Spend money freely on labour-saving appliances, so that you may be able to do with fewer servants. Avoid, however, the mistake of filling your rooms with too much furniture. Do not be wheedled by dealers into buying all manner of flimsy little tables and screens, and chairs that are not intended to be sat upon. Such things only harbour dust. The dignity and comfort of large airy rooms are much increased if they are furnished sufficiently but not lavishly with substantial articles which will stand ordinary usage. Let simplicity combined with comfort be your motto.

Social Ambitions.

THE man who has suddenly made money is always supposed to have great social ambitions; he is anxious, it is thought, to obtain a title, to go into Parliament, and to cut a figure in the eyes of his countrymen. Indeed, it generally happens that he does make the attempt to do some or all of these things, but as a rule he very hypocritically pretends that it is his wife who makes him, that she wants to be called "My lady" and to go into dinner before people who at one time would not have called upon her. This is generally very unjust to the poor woman. As a rule the social ambitions are all on the side of the man. I do not know how it would be in your case, my dear sir, but at any rate, if the ambitions are yours, I hope you will frankly admit it and not attribute them to your wife, unless she fully shares them.

It is certainly very curious to reflect that many a man who has made a great deal of money by shrewd business faculties seems, when once he is launched on the stormy waters of society, to be suddenly deprived of those very qualities to which he owes his prosperity. Too often he simply loses his head, and after squandering recklessly a great deal of money for a few weeks or a few months, suddenly goes to the opposite extreme and comes out as a first-class miser. The English of it generally is that he has found out one of his new friends in a mean trick of some kind, and this has the effect of making him bristle with suspicions, and put out his quills like an angry hedgehog.

I do not know whether you, my dear sir, ever build castles in the air, and amuse yourself by deciding what you would do if you were suddenly to become a millionaire, but at any rate it is to be hoped and believed that you would avoid these perils, which would certainly wreck your happiness as well as that of your wife.

Sudden Poverty.

It remains to consider the question of sudden poverty. In such circumstances, perhaps more than in any other, your wife will stand in need of your sympathy and consideration, for it is on her shoulders that much of the trouble will unavoidably fall. Only those who have tried to make a small income go a long way have any idea of the mental worry and torment of the operation, which resembles the proverbial attempt to squeeze a quart of liquid into a pint pot.

Sudden poverty resembles sudden wealth in one respect—namely, in the necessity for keeping a cool head, while it is superior to wealth in one respect—namely, in the remarkable insight which it gives you into the characters of your friends. After all, it is only poor men who know who are their real friends, and I have always thought that one great reason why so many millionaires lead, as we know they lead, unhappy lives, is because they are haunted by doubts about everybody around them, because they find it hard to have any confidence in human nature, and because they are ever suspecting baseness even where it does not exist. At any rate, a poor man is freed from that terror, though it must be admitted that not much else can be said for him by way of consolation.

How to bear Reverses.

AT the same time, there are many ways of bearing poverty, and you will find, I am convinced, that if you have to bear it, it is better to do so with dignity and without complaining. You will thereby enlist more sympathy in the end and more practical help from others than if, as so many people do, you are perpetually whining and lamenting over your fallen fortunes. It is hardly ever too late to face the effort to retrieve your circumstances, and if you take your wife fully into your confidence, and consult with her the best course to pursue, you will have the best chance of success. Indeed, it may well be that you may actually live to bless the day when poverty came to you, if it has brought you nearer to her, and cemented the bonds of loving affection and regard which unite you.

CHAPTER X.

IN SICKNESS AND IN HEALTH.

These words are apt to be spoken glibly enough on the solemn occasion of the marriage service, but people seldom realize the full meaning of the words, or how much they may have to bear in the future. The bridegroom very likely thinks (if he thinks about the matter at all) that his wife is strong and well, and will always be so.

In Sickness and in Health.

The Weakness of Women.

As a matter of fact, it is on you, my dear sir, that your wife's health will mainly depend. It is very difficult for men to realize how much weaker even quite strong women are than themselves. Often a husband will expect his wife to undergo what is for her great physical exertion, although she may not be at all ailing or weakly by comparison with the general run of her sex.

I know at least one very sad case in which the wife's health was really broken for years by the passion which her husband had for taking long walks. He was a man of the best possible intentions; he simply had no idea that the ten or fifteen miles which he could accomplish without any fatigue were far too much for a girl who was born and bred in a great city, and had probably never walked more than two miles at a stretch in her life before. She was too fond of him to remonstrate, and so the mischief was done.

You must be careful to watch for the first signs of fatigue, and always let your wife's strength rather than your own be the measure of the active exercise which you take together. Bicycling, of course, is not so likely to fatigue a woman as excessive walking, though a good deal even of that can be very injurious to a girl who is not accustomed to covering very long distances on her wheel.

Unwillingness to Complain.

It is a curious fact that the modern woman seldom or never complains of her health. I know a young lady who confessed occasionally for ten days or a fortnight to suffering from what she called slight muscular rheumatism. At the end of that time she was forced to give in and consult a doctor, who declared that she had all the time been suffering from severe pleurisy. Many other instances might be given of the pluck with which women will struggle on in the midst of real illness in order to avoid throwing up the sponge and laying up.

On the other hand, of course, there are a certain number of women who are apt to fancy themselves the victims of all manner of marvellous ailments when they are really suffering from nothing worse than a bad temper, or a disordered liver. I trust, however, that you, my dear sir, will not have married a woman of this kind, and, therefore, I say that you should keep an eye upon your wife's health, not only when she is ill, but with a view to preventing her from falling ill, and from overtaxing her strength in any direction.

"Days Off" for the Wife.

THERE was an old idea that the house-mother should never leave the house. Certainly there was a great deal to be said for it, and those old-fashioned house-wives undoubtedly did know how to make things very comfortable for their husbands and their brothers; but nowadays, when everybody travels so much more than they did, say fifty years ago, it does not seem so shocking to English feeling that the house-mother should occasionally take a holiday.

You will, I am convinced, find it a good plan to encourage your wife to go away occasionally for a few days at a time to stay with relations or friends, or even by herself, while you remain at home to take care of the children. You will find that this will have a most beneficial effect on her health in the great majority of cases. It may be said that the annual holiday at the seaside affords your wife as much change as she wants, but you must remember that that annual holiday involves a great deal of worry and work for her, and, indeed, if you think of it, is not a real holiday at all.

Health and Temper.

ANOTHER great point to consider is the influence which health has on

In Sickness and in Health.

temper. If you find after you are married that your wife develops a bad temper, or, if not absolutely a bad one, at any rate a querulous and complaining disposition, it will certainly be worth your while to consider whether it may not be due, in part at any rate, to a poor condition of health.

And here a word of warning should be given against quack remedies of various kinds, of which women are notoriously the greatest patrons. It is astonishing how many women of intelligence and education will believe whatever high-falutin' nonsense is advertised in the papers. Of course I do not mean that, because a box of pills or a liver mixture is widely advertised, it is therefore a delusion and a snare, but I do say that even the best of these preparations cannot possibly have the wonderful effects which are claimed for them by their enthusiastic proprietors.

It is partly for this reason that a good level-headed family doctor is so precious a possession, for he knows the individual requirements and the individual natures of the members of your household, which the compounder of much be-puffed pills and liver mixtures obviously does not. This is certainly a case in which a wise expenditure of money is cheaper in the end, though the doctor who charges his half-a-guinea a visit may seem so much less economical than the box of pills at 1s. 11½d.

Your own Health.

NOT less important than the state of your wife's health is your own, especially if, as is usually the case, you are the bread-winner of the family, and the domestic budget depends mainly, if not entirely, on your exertions. It is only common prudence, therefore, that you should take care of your health.

Of course I do not mean that you should be a faddist about it; a man may easily make himself ridiculous by perpetually taking his temperature and searching in medical books to find out what terrible ailment he fancies has smitten him. Yet even that is better than the criminal carelessness with which some men will sit in their wet clothes and ignore the dangers of damp boots. The terrible number of victims which consumption carries off every year in this country is greatly swollen by folly of this kind.

It is bad enough in the case of a man who is a bachelor and has practically no-one depending upon him for subsistence, but when a man marries he forfeits the privilege of making himself ill at his own sweet will and pleasure. Certainly one other life is closely involved in his, and probably there are other little lives too, for whose welfare he is responsible.

You must not, therefore, my dear sir, be deterred by any fear of ridicule, or by mere laziness, from taking those obvious and necessary precautions which will assuredly save you from expensive and troublesome illness, and will, moreover, promote your success in life. No employer, however sympathetic he may be at the time, really likes a man who is always falling ill, while, if you are a professional man, it is equally to your interest to be always at the service of your clients with both mind and body unimpaired.

Only a Cold.

The great Dr. Abernethy was once called in by a man's relations who were concerned about his health. The patient was very refractory, and said to Abernethy, "What nonsense it is to trouble you to come and see me; why! I have only got a cold." "A cold," said Abernethy, "what could you have worse?" And certainly it is too little understood that a cold, though it may be nothing in itself, is very often the beginning, and if neglected certainly the beginning, of serious disorder. Such simple precautions as keeping a pair of dry shoes at the office or place of business have saved many a man's life.

Fresh Air and Sunlight.

THE advantages of fresh air and sunlight, moreover, are not always as well understood in offices and places of business as they should be. It cannot be healthy to work for hours at a stretch in a room to which a sufficient amount of air is never admitted. Sunlight, especially in great towns, is often difficult to obtain, but nevertheless many offices actually take pains to exclude, by means of blinds and curtains, what little there is available, although science teaches us that there is no more powerful destroyer of disease-germs than the light of the sun.

CHAPTER XI.

THE FIRST BABY—AND THE LAST.

OF all the delights which fall to the lot of the average man, none ought to be more keen than the delight of contemplating and possessing his first baby.

False Shame.

MANY husbands and fathers have, I am afraid, the foolish idea that it is manly and altogether right and proper that they should affect indifference to their children until the little creatures are old enough to talk

The First Baby—and the Last. 175

and run about. Thus it was only the other day that a father wrote to one of the great London daily papers and declared that he only knew his own children from other children by their clothes. Few fathers of families have the excuse of the over-worked politician of whom it is related that in crossing St. James's Park one day, on his way to the House of Commons, he saw a beautiful child with its nurse. Withdrawing his mind from the cares of State, he stopped to admire the child, and asked the nurse who were its parents. "Well, sir," said the nurse, "Baby is yours!"

The great majority of fathers have plenty of time for making the acquaintance of their own children and certainly those who do are rewarded in many ways, not only in the increased affection with which their children regard them, but also in the higher links of love which are thereby forged between husband and wife.

The First Arrival.

INDEED, there is hardly any time in married life when the wife stands in so much need of your sympathy and of your affectionate interest as when she has her first baby. There may be some trifle of self-denial required on your part, for naturally a man does not take the same absorbing interest in infantile ailments as a woman

The First Baby —and the Last.

does, but if you look at the matter philosophically you will see that you ought to make every allowance for the charm and excitement of the first arrival. You may be sure that the subsequent ones will not arouse as much interest, though it may well be that you yourself may find your favourite among the later ones.

Don't Make Favourites.

I SAY the favourite with reference to your own private feelings. I do not, of course, mean that you should ever show any preference for one child over another; indeed, I would go so far as to say that there is scarcely a more fruitful source of ill-feeling in families than when the parents single out a particular child for special favours and special consideration. Children have a very keen sense of justice, which is most interesting to observe even in very early years, and though they may not, and probably will not, like to show any jealousy or discontentment, yet many a child has had his earlier years over-shadowed and made unhappy by the feeling that he was not liked by his parents as much as his more favoured brother or sister. Of course, the whole case is changed if one of the children is weakly or ailing. Its healthy brothers and sisters are quite capable of understanding the reason for favour in this case, and, indeed, they should be trained to show to the afflicted one special kindness and consideration, which will prove valuable lessons in after life.

In the Nursery.

As to the management of children in general, most people have their own ideas, and unfortunately it sometimes happens that the ideas of husband and wife do not coincide. Should this unhappily be the case with you, I advise you to be very careful not to let the children see that you and your wife do not see eye to eye with regard to them. In such a case you must talk over the matter with your wife in private, and perhaps by each of you yielding on some little point, you will be able to arrange a working compromise.

Of course it is always open to you to insist upon having your own way altogether, and ignoring your wife's wishes whenever they conflict with your own. She would probably submit if she saw that you were determined to carry your point, but it would not increase her affection for you. After all you must remember that, of the two, she is with the children much more than you are, and it is obviously desirable that she should have her heart in whatever system of management is adopted.

Beware of Systems.

This word system is a convenient one to use, but it should not be taken to mean any hard and fast, iron-bound rules. Much harm is done to children every day by the persistent carrying out of some hide-bound theory, indeed I rather think that the best system of all is the absence of any system. Of course there must be some rules in every household, but they must be based on reason, and care must be taken to prevent them from seeming arbitrary and useless to the children who have to obey them, and in this matter children are often sharper witted than their parents give them credit for.

Perhaps the most useful piece of advice that can be given to parents is to see as much of their children as possible. No nurse, however affectionate and competent, can ever take the place of the natural guardians; nurses, even the best of them, are often very ignorant, and they may do irreparable harm to the sensitive child-natures with the kindest of intentions. Moreover, in such matters as manners and behaviour, they are not the best possible guides, and they are apt to instil into the children false ideas of gentility, and so on, while of course thoroughly believing that their instruction is perfectly sound.

Keep the Children Quiet.

WHILE the children are still quite young, it is a good thing not to let them see much of your outside friends who come to the house. It is very difficult for grown-up people to realise how delicate and easily over-tired the brain of a child is, and visitors, from ignorance of how to treat children, often annoy and distress them very much. It often happens that after a child has seen a number of visitors and has been irritated by their clumsy familiarities, it has a crying fit which is put down to naughtiness, but which is really the result of sheer fatigue of brain. The mind of a child generally lags behind the development of its body, and it may undergo physical exertion much greater in amount than mental. But of course, if the parents study their children and are with them constantly, they will be able to tell pretty accurately how much of both bodily and mental exertion can be endured without injury.

Piccaninnies and the 'Puff=Puff.'

WHILE I am on this point, I will add a word of warning as to the imprudence of taking very young children on railway journeys. The fatigue of a railway journey is often, especially if there are many changes, as much as an adult can bear, and you, my dear sir, should see to it that

The First Baby—and the Last. 185

while your children are quite young, they are sheltered as much as possible from the strain and constant shocks to the nerves which a railway journey of any length must involve. Unfortunately we cannot all travel luxuriously in Pullman cars, and a third-class railway carriage is not the place in which a young child should be found unless it is absolutely necessary.

Nature's Way.

As a general rule, the principle of managing children should be to manage them as little as possible. I mean that they should be allowed to develop naturally on their own lines, and the attention of their parents should be directed to the removing of obstacles from their growth, both mental and physical.

Above all, they should never be forced to learn too soon. In this age of examinations and competition, it is a great temptation for the parents of clever children to bring them on in their lessons prematurely. But you must remember, my dear sir, that this is a great mistake, and really defeats its own object, for the little brain which is prematurely developed is only too apt to collapse, and then the child, who if more rationally treated would have grown up possessed of good abilities, relapses into rather a dull boy or girl. The matter concerns you in a special degree, for you must not forget that when mothers collect together for conversation and tea, they are very apt to boast of the achievements of their offspring.

Hence you must watch carefully to see that your wife is not led away, by the desire that her children should excel other children, into having them taught too soon, and making them precocious.

When to begin Lessons.

I THINK myself that it would be a good thing if, in ordinary cases, all lessons were postponed until the age of seven, but to many people that will no doubt seem too late. The question must depend to a great extent on the tastes of the individual child. For example many children teach themselves to read without any compulsion by the fresh interest they take in such things as advertisement hoardings and notice-boards, which provide large type letters combined in an attractive form. There is no harm in allowing a child to learn in this easy way, for nature herself sets the limit to lessons of this kind. Whatever direct instruction is given before the age of seven, you should see to it that it is extremely short and perfectly adapted to the childish intellect, and all the time you should be on the alert for the first sign of brain-weariness and discontent with the lessons which does not arise from mere naughtiness, that is, you should be prepared at any moment to cut off the lessons entirely.

The Last Arrival.

THERE remains the question of the last baby, who is sure to be almost as much a marvel in its way as the first. What you must guard against in his case is the danger of spoiling him, a danger which is greater than in the case of the first baby, for the youngest has all the adoring affection of his elder brothers and sisters in addition to that of his parents. It is the Benjamin of the family who runs the greatest risk of being spoilt.

Spoiling.

This brings us to the general question of spoiling. Shrewd observers have noticed that it is invariably other people's children who are spoilt, but seriously, it is a difficult thing for affectionate parents to avoid. Moreover, it must be remembered that what is ordinarily called spoiling has many degrees, and whether it is bad or not depends to a great extent on the nature of the particular child. If the child is sensitive, affectionate, warm-hearted, and naturally unselfish, then what is ordinarily called spoil-

The First Baby—and the Last.

ing will probably not do him very much harm. It is where there is a certain element of vanity, cruelty, and egotism in a child's nature that spoiling does harm. Perhaps it may be useful to describe the ideal child, and then every parent can estimate how very nearly their own offspring approach to that perfection of type.

The Ideal Child.

THE ideal child is modest and retiring, yet not affectedly shy; obedient, silent and reserved, except when spoken to by his elders; considerate to the feelings of other children, ever willing to give up toy or cake ; not over addicted to jam and other infantile vices; and above all, never guilty of anything like whining. In fact the ideal child is a little lady or gentleman in miniature, with polite manners and a perfectly clear sense of his or her comparative unimportance.

CHAPTER XII.

THE RIFT WITHIN THE LUTE.

To anyone who reflects upon the institution of marriage as it should be, there is hardly anything more tragic than the drifting apart of husband and wife. It happens mostly, I think, in middle age, when the pleasures and amusements in which young people delight begin to pall, and the creature comforts which support old age have not yet begun to be appreciated. Although, of course, there are many men whose feelings are very sensitive, yet, as a rule, the greatest pain of the separation falls on the wife, partly because women do, as a matter of fact, feel these things on the whole more than men, and partly because the husband has distractions and other resources which his wife probably has not.

The Children.

The rift generally arises with regard to the children, about their careers, their schools, and their matrimonial engagements. You have a son who is a little wild or idle, and you are, perhaps, inclined to be stern with him, while his mother, naturally enough, will not listen to a word against her darling boy. Or your

The Rift within the Lute.

daughter wishes to take up some profession which is open to women, and you are inclined to indulge her, but her mother would rather that she stayed at home to attend to her parents.

In such cases, which seem unfortunately only too common nowadays, it is extremely hard to suggest any remedy, for the difficulty is not generally one which can be compromised in any way. For that reason, therefore, my advice is that you make up your mind, not quickly, not without careful consideration, not without taking the advice of some trusted and wise friend, but that when you have made up your mind what to do, you should do it thoroughly. The great thing to avoid is letting things drift along in an unsatisfactory state of domestic irritation.

If the result of your deliberations is that you still disagree with your wife about the matter, she would much rather, I think, that you told her so kindly but firmly, explaining to her at the same time that it is not a matter in which you can please both sides. Let her feel, whichever way the matter is decided, that when once it is decided there can be no going back, and that it will be useless to attempt to alter your decision. That is the only way in which domestic peace can be restored. Even that may fail, but at any rate it is better than an unsatisfactory policy of drift, varied by occasional squabbles.

If your Wife grows Dowdy.

CONSIDERABLE indignation was aroused not very long ago when a middle-aged man, whose wife was also not young, had the bad taste to state in print that she was not "an improving property," as if he expected her to increase in value with time like a butt of old port. The man's frankness, however, does suggest a rather unfortunate characteristic of many women—a characteristic which frequently produces that "rift within the lute," which it is so desirable to avoid—I mean the tendency to relapse into dowdiness.

There is probably no other country in the world in which married women so quickly throw up the sponge and relapse into dowdiness as here. Thus it often happens that a woman, who is still on the right side of forty, will persist in dressing herself as if she were fifty, or even older, and unless her husband is absolutely devoted to her, or else very unobservant, he is apt to think less of her in consequence than he used to.

This unfortunately too common state of affairs arises generally from a false notion that, when once a woman has two or three children, there is something that savours of impropriety in her trying to look at all attractive any longer. It is wrongly supposed that she ought to consider herself a steady and rather dull matron, but this is a complete mistake, and you will do well, my dear sir, to prevent your wife, when the time comes, from putting herself on the shelf in this way.

To every Age its Charm.

The charm of womanhood does not depend on age, for we all of us know old ladies with white hair who are far more bright and charming than many young girls. Indeed, the truth is that every age of womanhood has its own special charm, and the intermediate stage is not the least to be admired. Indeed, your wife ought then to look in some ways at her best, for her children are growing up, she is perfectly sure of her position in the world, and I hope we may assume, my dear sir, that she is secure in the affection of her husband.

I do not, of course, mean that a woman of five-and-thirty or so should ape the graces of a young girl, or should dress herself like a bread-and-butter Miss, but there is a medium in all things, and she ought certainly not to betake herself to dowdy bonnets and funereal raiment. After all she is quite a young matron, as matrons go, and you must take an intelligent interest in her clothes and hats, her boots and gloves.

Every age pays for dressing, as the phrase goes, in its own way, and with your critical eye you may assist your wife materially in arriving at just that happy medium between skittishness and dowdiness in dress. In this way you may still go on being your wife's lover, proud of her and glad to see her admired, and so avoid a fruitful cause of "rifts within the lute." This is especially the case nowadays when, thanks to athletics, women lead healthier lives than of yore, and consequently retain a look of youthfulness much longer.

That Intimate Female Friend.

Another great cause of "rifts within the lute" is when the wife, now arrived at middle age, insists upon making a very intimate friend of some woman. This is likely to be particularly disagreeable to you, and it is not easy to advise you as to the best way of meeting the difficulty. It is very annoying to you to have a kind of sub-lieutenant of your wife's always about the house, probably interfering in matters which do not concern her, and giving advice perpetually where it is not wanted.

I trust that matters will never come to such a pass with you, but if they do, I can only urge you to deal gently and patiently with the matter. Consider with yourself whether you have not perhaps been a little lacking in affection towards your wife. A woman's heart is an inscrutable thing, and it may well be that she has made up her mind that she is losing your regard, and, in the recoil, she has thrown herself into the arms of this woman friend. Be at the pains to try and disabuse her of this notion, and you will probably find that the visits of the obnoxious friend will become fewer and fewer.

It is well, in a case like this, to avoid anything like an open explanation for as long as possible, but, if everything else fails, then you should certainly make your wife understand that, after all, she owes her first duty to you, and that you do not approve of the new friendship she has formed. If you make this explanation with gentleness and consideration for her feelings, it is most likely that all will go right, for you may be sure that she knows in her heart that what you say is true, and that, by comparison with her love for you, her love for her friend is nothing.

A Lack of Interests in Common.

THE most hopeless case of all is, I think, when husband and wife drift apart, after some years of married life,

The Rift within the Lute.

because they had originally no common interests—at any rate none strong enough to endure the test of marriage. If this should be your case, you are indeed to be pitied, for it is scarcely possible to advise anything but a patching up of the difficulty.

In such a case the difference between husband and wife is too radical and too deep-seated for them really to be brought together again, but what I would urge is that an open separation should, at any rate, be avoided. It is an ignominious thing for two grown-up people who have entered upon the serious step of marriage to confess before all the world that they have made a failure of it, and if they have children then it is all the more necessary for them to avoid anything like an open scandal.

Drifting Apart.

THERE is seldom anything like a real quarrel in these cases, it is rather that in each person's mind there dawns the conviction that a complete mistake has been made in the marriage, and that the congenial companionship till the day of death which marriage ought to bring is out of the question. So there is no open breach and, as I have said, husband and wife simply drift apart. There is nothing for them to do but to take the consequences, and to remain together on as

The Rift within the Lute.

friendly terms as they can for the sake of their children, if they have any, and for the sake of their relations.

A working arrangement is often arrived at by the illness of one or other of the parties. After all, the pain and distress of a fellow-creature appeal to us all more or less poignantly, and they may even form a golden bridge by which husband and wife, who have drifted apart may be re-united on what are, outwardly at least, the old terms of affection.

Nagging in both Sexes.

I HAVE left to the last what is, I am convinced, on the whole the most potent destroyer of connubial happiness—namely, nagging. It is always assumed to be a peculiarly feminine vice, and certainly I would earnestly implore any lady who does me the honour of reading these pages to be perpetually on her guard against falling into it.

But I am forced to recognise the fact that male naggers are much too common, and I think it is because many men do not realise that the domestic life cannot be conducted on the same lines as those of the office or the place of business. It is necessary for a business man to be firm and strict with those who work for him or under him. He is obliged to regard their performances with a somewhat critical eye.

Leave it on the Doorstep.

UNFORTUNATELY many men bring this fault-finding disposition home with them, and, by applying it indiscriminately to wife and children, merely succeed in driving peace and happiness away from their door. It is not worth while from any point of view. I suppose you do not, my dear sir, regard your wife as a sort of upper servant or managing clerk. Yet on no other theory would you be justified in treating her to the perpetual stream of embittering criticism and fault-finding to which some men treat their wives.

Never forget that women are far more sensitive to words, and especially to sarcastic words, than men are. It is much less trouble in the end to lead a woman than to drive her. Whatever worries you may have outside your home, see that you always leave them on the doorstep. For there is something sacred about the home, and angry, cruel words are as unseemly within its walls as they would be in church. Let there be perpetual peace in your home, so far as you can insure it.

Two to make a Quarrel.

You may ask, "But what am I to do if my wife is the nagger?" Well,

The Rift within the Lute. 211

you know the old proverb that it takes two to make a quarrel, and I think you will find that silence is your best weapon. At the same time, though in the case we have supposed your wife "goes on at" you unreasonably, it might be worth while to consider whether there is not some ground for her complaints. Perhaps she has a mania for tidiness, and you have a habit of leaving your things all over the house.

In that case you should watch to find her in an amiable mood and then propose a compromise to her—that she on her side should agree to be less particular about putting things away, and that you on your side should try to be more so. Remember that there is no really successful marriage without perpetual give-and-take of this kind, and that is why you will often see old married people who have grown as like one another in tastes and disposition as two tabby cats.

CHAPTER XIII.

DARBY AND JOAN.

The universal popularity of the famous old song is an indication of the extent to which the idea of union throughout a long married life has seized upon the popular imagination. Although it is an ideal, yet there is no lack of elderly couples whose deep connubial affection testifies to the fact that it is an ideal which is perfectly possible of attainment.

I may perhaps be pardoned for thinking that one method, at any rate, of securing the realization of this charming picture of old age spent in mutual love and esteem, is to follow the advice offered in these pages as the result of no small experience and observation.

The Art of Growing Old.

It is certainly an art to grow old gracefully, and the real secret is, I think, to see that your heart retains the freshness of youth, though your body may gradually grow less and less upright and the snows of old age may whiten your hair.

Whether your wife grows old gracefully too, will depend on you almost entirely. Do not—I will not say neglect her—but do not slacken one whit of your attentions and little observances because she loses the bloom of youth—that youth which she gave to you, and for which she should be repaid by steady and increasing love and regard.

Elderly people are often inclined to allow themselves to be put on the shelf too early. It is partly their own fault, for, though they may think that young people are very selfish and inconsiderate, yet they should ask themselves whether they have not contributed to this result by ceasing to keep up any fresh interest in the young people's doings. Every age of man has its own besetting form of selfishness, and when people are growing old they can best fight against the special selfishness of age by forcing themselves, if need be, to sympathize with the ambitions and interests of the young people around them. In this way you and your Joan may renew your youth and retain the fond affection of those around you until the end of your lives.

Age should Sympathize with Youth.

It is to be feared that many old people die unwept and unlamented even by those who should be their nearest and dearest, simply from an inability to realize that old age has its duties as well as its privileges. Anything like querulousness is especially to be avoided. Young people are naturally impatient; to them the world with all its fascinating possibilities lies stretched out like some beautiful landscape; and though you may feel, now that you are nearing the end of your stage, that life is after all more sad than joyful, yet it would be cruel for you to damp the ardour of fresh young enthusiasm by any pessimistic croakings.

The effort to maintain this fresh interest in the world around you, and especially in the young, will not be a hard one for long, if indeed it is hard at all. You will soon find that the reward is great, and that young people will readily respond to the sympathy of their elders. You may, too, have the satisfaction of helping them now and again with judicious words of counsel, based upon your knowledge of life, and you will find that they will take heed to such words far more readily if they have already had experience of your interest and sympathy in their doings. Unfortunately it generally happens that those old people who are most free with their advice are just those who look upon the doings of the young in a spirit of carping criticism, not unmixed with secret and petty envy.

Elderly People's Recreations.

Of course you and your wife, as you grow old together, will naturally have to give up, one by one, many of the recreations and amusements of your prime, but it is a mistake to give these up too soon. The time comes when you are too easily fatigued, both of you, to join with young people in expeditions and similar amusements.

Many people, when the time comes, give up going about altogether, because they feel that they play the part of skeletons at the banquet; but there is no reason why Darby and Joan should not toddle about quietly together, away from the more energetic exertions of younger people. I know more than one elderly couple who have not given up by any means their zest for travelling and seeing still more of the wonderful world around them, though, with great good sense, they abstain from the temptation to take with them young people who would only be bored by their necessarily deliberate methods.

The famous French statesman, Talleyrand, regarded a knowledge of the game of whist as an absolutely necessary provision for old age. Unfortunately there seems, as a rule, to be something peculiarly irritating to old people in this otherwise excellent game; though, to be sure, it affords an admirable discipline for the temper. Moreover, it has the disadvantage of requiring four players. But there are many other games, from chess downwards, at which Darby and Joan can play in the quiet winter evening of their lives. The great thing is to keep up as many keen interests and occupations as possible as you are growing old, especially if they are such as you can share with your wife. For remember that it is on her that you ultimately depend for companionship more than on anyone else, as you go down the hill of life together, and, therefore, you should do all in your power to cultivate all those tastes and pursuits which you have in common with her.

Physical Weakness.

THE approach of old age generally brings with it more or less considerable physical weakness, if not actual illness. There may be a certain amount of pain for you and your wife to bear, and it is very necessary that you should bear it with fortitude and with as little complaining as possible. How often do we see old people who are ailing complain all the time and even exaggerate their sufferings.

The result is that they give their children and others round them great anxiety and sorrow for a time, but, as time goes on, it is not in human nature to keep up the perpetual sympathy that is needed. So the old people find, as the sands of their life run out, that the affection of those around them has gone, and that it is only a feeling of duty on the part of their relations which preserves them from being ministered to by strangers. There is nothing which kills affection and esteem so quickly as constant complaining. Indeed, it has been known to turn love not only into indifference but into actual hatred.

Do not, therefore, fall into this error. Let your complaints be few and less than proportionate to your pain. You need not fear that there will be in consequence any failure of attention and care. Those round you have sharper eyes, perhaps, than you think, and if you do not wring their hearts with the tale of your sufferings, you may be sure that they will understand and be grateful for your forbearance.

CHAPTER XIV.

SECOND MARRIAGES.

A General Prejudice.

There is a very general prejudice against second marriages, especially against the re-marriage of a widow. For my part I hardly think there is quite sufficient ground for this feeling, although no doubt circumstances do render it in particular cases entirely justifiable. But, as a rule, if a widow or a widower marries again, of course after a proper interval, it is surely more reasonable to regard the step as an implied compliment to the husband or wife who is dead, for the second marriage, if it means anything at all, means that the first union was so happy and so successful that the survivor feels a natural inclination for the estate of matrimony itself.

Of course, I know there are many gloomy-minded people who would prefer that the survivor of a happy union should spend the remaining years on earth in grieving for the dead, but in all probability this would be the very last thing that the one who has gone before would desire.

Making your Will.

The question of second marriages can hardly help affecting you, my dear sir, in some way or other, even though you should never yourself contract a union of this kind. For instance, the question will have to be considered when you make your will, which you should do as soon as possible after you are married because, as is well known, the marriage contract invalidates all wills previously made.

In making your will you will inevitably have to contemplate the contingency that your widow may marry again. However firmly you are convinced in your secret heart that she would not dream of taking such a step, still you would be well advised to make provision for it, for you cannot possibly tell how circumstances may be altered by your death.

Many husbands leave all their property to their wives on condition that there is no re-marriage. This has always seemed to me scarcely a fair thing to do, unless it is felt that the wife needs special protection against the wiles of fortune-hunters. Even that excuse is rather thin now-a-days, when married women have absolute control in law over their property and the once-flourishing occupation of fortune-hunting has experienced a considerable depression.

Humiliating Conditions.

AFTER all, the circumstance that your wife consented to marry you may justly be regarded, by you at any rate, as some sign of her good judgment, and you probably will not do wrong in most cases if you leave to your widow whatever provision seems suitable for her without attaching any conditions to the bequest.

Naturally enough, the prospect of some plausible stranger worming his way into the confidence of your widow, and leading a lazy existence as her second husband on the fruits of your fore-sight and prudence, is not very pleasant for you to contemplate. But, on the other hand, to impose any condition or restraint on her second marriage is rather too much like proclaiming to the world, either that you feel you cannot trust your wife's common-sense, or that you are obliged to bribe her, so to speak, to cherish your memory.

Either way the look of the thing is bad, and so, on the whole, unless your wife is exceptionally lacking in sense and knowledge of her fellow-creatures, you will do well to attach no ignominious conditions on her inheritance.

Act with Consideration.

IF, however, you reject this advice and make the condition alluded to, at any rate let it be so arranged that, if she becomes a widow a second time, she shall resume the enjoyment of the full income.

It may be worth while to remember, however, that if you attach a condition restraining your widow from re-marrying, you immediately give certain other persons a strong interest in making her marry again, as in that case they would benefit. Such a clause would probably expose her to the greatest annoyance and pain, especially as, where money is at stake, even very reputable people often behave in a manner of which they ought to be thoroughly ashamed.

You certainly do not, I presume,

desire that your will should become a bone of contention and a source of bitterness and misunderstandings after your death. Probably almost every will disappoints somebody, but the best way to reduce the disappointment to a *minimum* is to leave what you have to leave to the people you wish to benefit absolutely and without tying them down by any conditions. It is on conditions in wills that lawyers grow fat.

Choosing a Second Wife.

It may be that you have been left a widower after having experienced the happiness of a thoroughly united marriage. In your loneliness it may

Second Marriages. 233

well seem that you stand in even greater need of the congenial companionship and comfort of matrimony than you did when you were a bachelor, and so, without for a moment intending any disrespect to the memory of your late wife, but rather believing that it is what she would wish you to do, you decide to take the step of making a second marriage. What principles should guide you in the choice of a second wife? Certainly they will be different, almost inevitably, from those which guided you in your first choice.

Some people have a perfect mania for finding what they imagine to be suitable second wives for widowers.

It will be well to steer clear of these managing folk, unless you place real confidence in their judgment. Generally speaking, it is not wise to take advice on the matter—at any rate not directly. It is better to proceed cautiously, not giving yourself away, but ascertaining as much as possible in a quiet way about the lady's nature, temper, disposition, and how she is regarded in her own circle. This is all the more necessary if you are contemplating a marriage of prudence rather than of inclination.

"For the Sake of the Children."

PROBABLY you have several children to be considered, and, though you must not sacrifice your own feelings entirely to them, still you cannot help recognizing that they ought to be thought of in the matter. Many second marriages are contracted by widowers against their own inclination, and entirely for the sake of their children. This is especially the case when the widower has no sister, or mother, or other near relation to keep house for him and to look after the little ones.

It is better, if you can, to make your second marriage, if you make one at all, either when your children are very young or when they are almost, if not quite, grown up. It is in the intermediate stage that children most often suffer from a step-mother. Your object must be to make the new arrangement run as smoothly as possible, and to secure for the new-comer in your household as warm a welcome as you can.

To that end it is important that you should tell your children yourself about your contemplated marriage, but, I need hardly say, not until you have been definitely accepted by the lady. It may make a great difference to the way in which your children regard your step-mother if you tell them yourself, instead of leaving the task to some less sympathetic relation or friend. Do not be offended if they fail to receive the news with any great enthusiasm, for, if you try to put yourself in their place, you will see that it cannot help being to a certain extent a shock to them, and obviously it is desirable that you should do your best to lessen the shock.

The Lady's Age.

THE question of the lady's age is more important in the case of second marriages than of first ones, especially if there are children to be considered. Very rarely is it successful when a middle-aged or elderly widower marries quite a young girl. It is far better, if you can, to choose some one more nearly of your own age, whom the children can respect and look up to and quickly learn to love. It is a very false position for a young girl, as a rule, to become the wife of a man a good deal older than herself, especially if he has already a growing-up family. The circumstances must be very exceptional which would make such a union at all desirable.

The Evils of Gossip.

HAVING once chosen your second wife, you must stand by her through thick and thin. If necessary, you must even take her part against your own children. Most important is it to be on the look-out for foolish or ill-natured gossip. Dismiss at once any servant who talks to the young people about their step-mother, and check any relation who does so instantly.

The matter is not one which you should allow to be discussed for a moment. Whether your choice is a good or a bad one, it has been made, and you are not answerable for it to any interfering busybody. Great and irreparable harm is often done in families by foolish and reckless talk, and you must not forget that there is hardly a more fascinating subject to the average empty-headed gossip than a second marriage.

Widows as Second Wives.

It is safe to say that a good deal of the popular prejudice against widows, and of the general belief in their designing nature, is due to the elder Mr. Weller's famous warning to his son to beware of them. But Tony Weller was hardly in a position to give an impartial opinion, and you must not allow yourself to be influenced by it either way. Dickens's object was to draw a humorous and life-like picture of a typical English character, not to give advice for the practical affairs of life.

For my part, I think widows are often very hardly used. If they are still young and attractive they are apt to be suspected of matrimonial designs by the other sex, while by their own sex they are often treated with that subtle sort of unkindness which women do not scruple sometimes to practise on those they dislike. A widow is usually in a position which should command general sympathy. For one thing she is probably a good deal poorer than when her husband was alive, and naturally her whole life is more or less overshadowed by his loss. Even if she announces in the plainest language her resolve never to change her condition, no one believes her, and when, after the first grief of her bereavement is over, she begins timidly to distract her mind with the ordinary things of life, the gossips are sure to begin their ill-natured comments behind her back.

Widower and Widow.

On general grounds it would seem most natural and suitable that a widower should choose a widow as his second wife. Like him, she has known the bitterness of bereavement, and, as is well known, a similar sorrow is a wonderful link between two human hearts. Then there is the practical, work-a-day consideration that a woman who has already been married once has in all probability already acquired that domestic experience and tact which are so desirable in marriage. She has at any rate some knowledge of the masculine nature, and she has had an opportunity of revising in the light of experience any high-flown romantic ideals in which as a young girl she may have indulged. To put it crudely, she knows how to make a comfortable home for a man; she has a better notion of give-and-take and bear and forbear than a single woman, and any little roughnesses and angles in her disposition have been rounded off.

If, my dear sir, you should ever have an idea of marrying a widow, no doubt you will give due weight to these considerations, and you will be guided also by the particular circumstances of the case. At the same time I feel bound to express my opinion that, as a general rule, the marriage of a widower and a widow is to be deprecated, especially if both the lady and the gentlemen have children.

I have known an instance in which such a marriage turned out well, and where more children appeared on the scene and grew up amicably with the other two families. Such cases are, however, undoubtedly rare, and the risk of family disagreements is considerable. Moreover, a widow naturally has all her own ideas on the education and upbringing of children, which are pretty sure not to be quite the same as those of your first wife.

Undoubtedly if you have only one child the matter is greatly simplified ; or if your children are all boys the matter is easier, for, as a rule, boys get on better with a step-mother than girls do.

A Parting Word.

A PARTING word may not be out of place. It must be understood that the advice given in these pages is not intended to be applied to every particular case. My object has been to give what my experience teaches me is the most generally useful counsel in regard to those difficulties which are most commonly met with throughout life's journey. But I know only too well that the great problems of life are not easily solved.

THE END.

Mr. THOMAS BURLEIGH'S
New & Forthcoming Publications

THE PEN AND THE BOOK. Crown 8vo. 6s. By Sir Walter Besant.

THE QUEEN'S JUSTICE. Crown 8vo. 3s. 6d. By Sir Edwin Arnold.

CHRISTINA ROSSETTI: a Biographical and Critical Study. The Authorised Life. By Mackenzie Bell. With Six Portraits and Six Facsimiles, being all the original illustrations. Fourth Edition, completing two thousand five hundred copies. 6s.

PATERSON'S PARISH : A LIFE-TIME AMONG THE DISSENTERS. Crown 8vo 5s. By Dr. Joseph Parker.

THE PASSING OF PRINCE ROZAN : A ROMANCE OF THE SEA. Crown 8vo. Gilt Top. 6s. By John Bickerdyke.
   A strange and romantic yachting story, throwing, incidentally, considerable light on the methods of modern company promoters and the hired director.

HER WILD OATS. A Novel. 6s. By John Bickerdyke.
"Audaciously original and diverting."—*Daily Mail.*
"Quaint, humourous, and delightful."—*Truth.*

A TOUCH OF THE SUN. — A Novel. 6s. By Mrs. Aylmer Gowing.

THE WANDERING ROMANOFF. A Novel. Crown 8vo. 3s. 6d. By Bart Kennedy.

THE HISTORY OF A MAN : by the Man. 6s.

THE MORALS OF JOHN IRELAND. 1s. Cloth, 1s. 6d.

OLIVETTE. By A. V. 1s. *net.*

THE GULISTAN OF SA'DI. 3s. 6d. *net.* By Sir Edwin Arnold.

17, Cecil Court, Charing Cross Road.

Mr. THOMAS BURLEIGH'S
New and Forthcoming Publications.

GOD IS LOVE: A TALE OF THE ARDENNES. Crown 8vo. With Frontispiece. 3s. 6d. By T. Mullett Ellis.

STUDIES IN SOME FAMOUS LETTERS. 6s. By J. C. Bailey.

MAUREEN MOORE. 6s. By Rupert Alexander.

BALLYRONAN. New and Cheaper Edition. 3s. 6d. By Rupert Alexander.

THE VICAR OF ST. NICHOLAS. New and Cheaper Edition. 3s. 6d. By Rupert Alexander.

DENE FOREST SKETCHES. Second Series. 6s. By Rev. S. M. Tracey Boevey.

FRENCH AS SAID. 3s. 6d. *net.* By E. Aldred Williams.

MARIANNA, AND OTHER STORIES 6s. By Georgette Agnew.

JOHN THADDEUS MACKAY. 6s. By Charles Williams.

LAKHMI, THE RAJPUT'S BRIDE. 3s. 6d. *net.* By A. Rogers.

THE POPULAR HANDBOOK OF THE BRITISH CONSTITUTION. 6s. By J. Johnston.

DOT AND THE KANGAROO. By E. C. Pedley. Illus. 3s. 6d. *net.*

VERSES FOR GRANNIE SUGGESTED BY THE CHILDREN, and set down by S. M. Fox. Illus. 3s. 6d. *net.*

NINETY NORTH. 6s.

17, Cecil Court, Charing Cross Road.